Sustainable Finance

Sustainable Finance is a concise and authoritative reference series linking research and practice. It provides reliable concepts and research findings in the ever growing field of sustainable investing and finance, SDG economics and Leadership with the declared commitment to present the theories, methods, tools and investment approaches that can fulfil the United Nations Sustainable Development Goals and the Paris Agreement COP 21/22 alongside with de-risking assets and creating triple purpose solutions that ensure the parity of profit, people and planet through choice architecture passion and performance. The series addresses market failure, systemic risk and reinvents portfolio theory, portfolio engineering as well as behavioural finance, financial mediation, product innovation, shared values, community building, business strategy and innovation, exponential tech and creation of social capital. Sustainable Finance and SDG Economics series helps to understand keynotes on international guidelines, guiding accounting and accountability principles, prototyping new developments in triple bottom line investing, cost benefit analysis, integrated financial first plus impact first concepts and impact measurement. Going beyond adjacent fields (like accounting, marketing, strategy, risk management) it integrates the concept of psychology, innovation, exponential tech, choice architecture, alternative economics, blue economy shared values, professions of the future, leadership, human and community development, team culture, impact, quantitative and qualitative measurement, Harvard Negotiation, mediation and complementary currency design using exponential tech and ledger technology. Books in the series contain latest findings from research, concepts for implementation, as well as best practices and case studies for the finance industry.

This book series is indexed in SCOPUS.

Karen Wendt • Mathias Hauser

Green FinTech

Impact Taxonomy for Swiss Fintech

Springer

Karen Wendt
Sustainable Finance
Cham, Zug, Switzerland

Mathias Hauser
Frankfurt am Main, Germany

ISSN 2522-8285 ISSN 2522-8293 (electronic)
Sustainable Finance
ISBN 978-3-031-78278-7 ISBN 978-3-031-78279-4 (eBook)
https://doi.org/10.1007/978-3-031-78279-4

This Springer imprint is published by the registered company Springer Nature Switzerland AG
The registered company address is: Gewerbestrasse 11, 6330 Cham, Switzerland

Who Should Read This Book

The Impact Taxonomy is a powerful tool in making investment decisions, encouraging stakeholder engagement, facilitating training and capacity building, assisting portfolio construction, stimulating product innovation, managing risk, and supporting research & development within the Swiss and global fintech industry. Notably, it fosters stakeholder engagement by promoting a shared understanding of impact-driven fintechs, stimulates capacity-building efforts through a standardized impact measurement approach, and allows for more refined portfolio construction. Further, the taxonomy incentivizes product innovation by offering insight into sustainable practices and impact measurement and facilitates risk management by providing an understanding of fintech performance and associated investment risks.

Foreword

"One can see from space how the human race has changed the Earth. Nearly all of the available land has been cleared of forest and is now used for agriculture or urban development. The polar icecaps are shrinking and the desert areas are increasing. At night, the Earth is no longer dark, but large areas are lit up. All of this is evidence that human exploitation of the planet is reaching a critical limit. But human demands and expectations are ever-increasing. We cannot continue to pollute the atmosphere, poison the ocean and exhaust the land. There isn't any more available."

Physicist & Author — Stephen Hawking

Interview List Pre-Sample

Interview 1

Category: ☒ Association / ☐ VC-Fund
Date: Monday, 7 November 2022
Duration: 25:38 minutes
Place: Online Meeting

Interview 2

Category: ☐ Association / ☒ VC-Fund
Date: Wednesday, 9 November 2022
Duration: 21:10 minutes
Place: Online Meeting

Interview 3

Category: ☐ Association / ☒ VC-Fund
Date: Wednesday, 9 November 2022
Duration: 17:12 minutes
Place: Online Meeting

Interview Sample

Interview 1: Co-Founder, CEO at a leading Swiss Fintech

Category: ☒ Open Banking / ☐ Open Finance / ☐ Cybersecurity
Date: 13 February 2023
Duration: 53:01 minutes
Place: Online Meeting

Interview 2: Co-Founder of a leading Swiss Smart Bank

Category: ☒ Open Banking / ☐ Open Finance / ☐ Cybersecurity
Date: 24 February 2023
Duration: 01:02:10 minutes
Place: Online Meeting

Interview 3: Impact and ESG Specialists

Category: ☒ Open Banking / ☐ Open Finance / ☐ Cybersecurity
Date: 7 March 2023
Duration: 45:32 minutes
Place: Online Meeting

Interview 4: Co-Founder and Head of Investments at a leading Swiss Fintech

Category: ☒ Open Banking / ☐ Open Finance / ☐ Cybersecurity
Date: 24 March 2023
Duration: 42:36 minutes
Place: Online Meeting

Interview 5: Senior Business Development Manager at one of Switzerland's leading Impact Investment Managers (Impact Investing Expert)

Category: ☒ Open Banking / ☐ Open Finance / ☐ Cybersecurity
Date: 27 March 2023
Duration: 39:18 minutes
Place: Online Meeting

Editorial Introduction

The transformative arena of impact investing is witnessing significant shifts. Investors today have a significant exposure to the evolving landscape of impact investing, and the lack of standardization in the impact sphere has become a problem for investors, investment companies, institutional investors, and in particular fintechs, demonstrating an exigent need to construct a standardized Impact Taxonomy for Swiss Financial Institutions, Institutional Investors, and Fintechs alike that are using Artificial Intelligence (AI). NexGen Investors will use AI as a core element of their investment strategies, and traditional investment models will be superseded both from the customer side and the provider's perspective. The taxonomy we are proposing here is envisaged to create a uniform system, thereby enabling Swiss asset managers, wealth managers, financial institutions, and fintechs to quantify their impact in a standardized manner. The inherent heterogeneity in the asset management area when it comes to ESG and impact investing shows its aggregated effects in the fintech industry, so in particular the Open Banking and Open Finance sector necessitates the development of this taxonomy, which aims to enhance clarity, transparency, and comparability in measuring impacts, thus facilitating informed decision-making for investors, regulators, and the fintech entities themselves. This work is conceived as a response to the specified needs of this industry, substantiating a detailed examination and proposing a framework for an Impact Taxonomy tailored to the Swiss financial sector.

We started from the following questions:

1. Which determinants should an impact taxonomy for Swiss fintechs contain in order to categorize the generated impact uniformly?
2. What methods can be used to collect evidence-based impact and ESG data in the fintech industry?

First of all, our Fintech definition also included the financial institutions and asset managers who are proactively using AI and technology to define, implement, and control their investment thesis and strategies. A rigorous analytical approach has been adopted to answer these crucial questions, the responses to which form the bedrock of the proposed Impact Taxonomy. This methodological rigor is underpinned by an interdisciplinary approach, synthesizing key insights from leading Swiss impact-driven fintechs as well as ESG and Impact professionals. The work in front of you therefore is a synthesis of research on secondary data in combination with the creation of primary data through interviews with ESG and impact professionals, which then was subjected to a quantitative analysis in order to get robust results.

The research commences by conducting a thorough examination of the existing literature and resources pertaining to Impact Investing. Furthermore, an investigation into pre-existing measurement standards to assess the impact generated by fintechs in the context of Open Banking and Open Finance is undertaken. To identify best-in-class fintechs operating in the domain of Open Banking and Open Finance, qualitative pre-interviews have been conducted with industry experts as part of a market sounding. These interviews serve as a crucial step in selecting the best-in-class fintechs for further analysis. The main phase of the project employs a mixed-methods approach, combining qualitative and quantitative methodologies. Qualitative interviews are conducted with representatives from fintech companies as well as Impact and ESG experts. The primary objective of these interviews is to gain insights into the current practices employed by these organizations in collecting Impact and ESG Data. Additionally, the interviews aim to identify relevant criteria that can contribute to the establishment of an impact taxonomy. In addition to the expert interviews, a thorough desk research is conducted to formulate an initial concept of an impact taxonomy. These efforts result in the creation of a framework that categorizes and classifies the impact generated by fintechs, aligning it with predefined Impact Themes, Strategic Objectives, and Key Performance Indicators (KPIs). Once the impact taxonomy has been developed, a quantitative survey has been conducted to evaluate the effectiveness of the identified Impact Themes, Strategic Objectives, and KPIs. To ascertain the significance and reliability of the impact taxonomy, an in-depth statistical analysis is performed. This analysis enables a robust evaluation of the Impact Taxonomy, providing insights into its validity and applicability.

Without pre-empting the content of this work, we like to highlight some very interesting results here and hope you will enjoy the entire journey on how we came to our conclusions.

As we applied both a bottom-up approach to find out about relevant Key Performance Indicators and a top-down approach where indicators were defined using the literature available on the topic we were able to compare the results of these two approaches. It was therefore interesting to find out that the bottom-up approach using the criteria of experts in the field performed better overall, compared to the top-down approach with criteria found in the literature on the fintech level.

KPIs assessing user satisfaction generally score lower within their respective impact themes, suggesting user satisfaction isn't a main driver for impact. This seems to be a new and important finding, as impact has often been conceptualized as increasing customer satisfaction and being a proxy for sustainability.

The bottom-up approach analysis shows high relevance for "Innovation" and "Sustainability". Other factors like "Financial Inclusion", "Financial Literacy", "Transparency", "Affordability", and "Efficiency" have a linear cumulative relevance trend with the second highest score displaying the highest frequency, meaning these values are important to users and to fintechs alike.

It is interesting to see that innovation and sustainability alongside transparency show positive or at least linear effects, while “Economic Growth”, “Personalization”, and “Security” demonstrate a flatter trend.

“Financial Resilience” has high relevance despite low scores, while “Gender Equality” has medium relevance. Despite not aligning perfectly with a Gaussian distribution, an approximate normal distribution was assumed through a comprehensive Q-Q plot analysis. The Levene’s test suggested variance homogeneity between Open Banking and Open Finance.

Using Backward Stepwise Regression, the study found age significantly impacts “Financial Inclusion”, “Financial Literacy”, “Transparency”, “Affordability”, and “Sustainability”, and the Swiss canton influences “Innovation” in Open Banking. Both age and Swiss canton affect “Gender Equality” and “Financial Resilience”, but no significant influences were found for “Efficiency”, “Personalization”, “Security”, and “Economic Growth”. The top-down approach showed that sustainability-related groups significantly influenced Economic, Technological, Regulatory, and Collaboration Factors, but not Environmental, Social, and Governance Factors.

We hope you will enjoy this book’s journey as much as we did in creating it.

Karen Wendt
Mathias Hauser

Contents

About the Authors

Karen Wendt is the President of Sustainable Finance (Cham, Switzerland) and CEO of ECCOS Impact GmbH (Cham, Switzerland). She is also a serial entrepreneur, scientist and co-editor of the Sustainable Finance book series at Springer. She advises companies on sustainability and is proven expert in impact investing, international management, sustainable finance, and strategy development. She is currently conducting research on social entrepreneurship, stock exchanges and portfolio engineering.

Mathias Hauser is a highly educated finance professional with expertise in mergers & acquisitions (M&A), corporate finance, private equity investment controlling, and capital markets. He is currently working on his M.Sc. in Finance at the Frankfurt School of Finance Management (Germany).

List of Abbreviations

AuM	Assets Under Management
EIA	Environmental Impact Assessment
ESG	Environment – Social – Governance
EU	European Union
FAO	Food and Agriculture Organization
GIIN	Global Impact Investing Network
GIIRS	Global Impact Investing Ratings System
GOGLA	Global Off-Grid Solar Energy Association
GRI	Global Reporting Initiative
HIA	Health Impact Assessment
IFC	International Finance Corporation
IMM	Impact Measurement and Management
IMP	Impact Management Project
IRIS+	Impact Reporting and Investment Standards
KPI	Key Performance Indicator
OECD	Organization for Economic Co-operation and Development
PRI	Principles for Responsible Investment
SDGs	Sustainable Development Goals
SEA	Strategic Environmental Assessment
SIA	Social Impact Assessment
SPTF	Social Performance Task Force
SRI	Socially Responsible Investing
UN	United Nations
UNEP FI	United Nations Environment Programme Finance Initiative

List of Figures

List of Tables

Introduction to WHY Fintechs Need a Taxonomy

1

1 Background

In recent years, the importance of sustainability, ESG criteria, and Impact Investing has undergone a notable increase, both at the corporate and national levels as well as on a global scale. Especially the field of Impact Investing has increasingly become a major subject of research and practice. Unfortunately, there is a lack of scientifically founded knowledge of a uniform and standardized measuring of the impact of fintechs. At the same time, humanity is faced with the necessity of adapting to the limited resources of planet Earth and an unprecedented global trend towards a holistic approach to sustainability has emerged, affecting economic, social, and ecological dimensions. Many different systems, including, but not limited to, transportation, healthcare, education, food, and finance necessitate a fundamental reassessment and reimagining. In view of the task of realizing far-reaching changes within the financial system, impact investments constitute a central leverage point (Wendt, 2018, p. ix). The financial industry assumes a critical role in realizing the objectives outlined in the UN 2030 agenda and the Paris Agreement. Most importantly, digital finance innovations have proven their capability to help enable a transition towards more sustainable business models in the financial sector. However, considerable additional investments amounting to at least $3 trillion each year across the globe, with $1.4 trillion allocated to developing nations, are required for the effective implementation of the Paris Agreement and the achievement of the Sustainable Development Goals (SDGs) (Puschmann et al., 2020, p. 1).

K. Wendt, M. Hauser, *Green FinTech*, Sustainable Finance,
https://doi.org/10.1007/978-3-031-78279-4_1

2 Initial Situation

This research aims to furnish a comprehensive survey of the existing body of literature concerning impact taxonomies and measurement instruments, while concurrently formulating a preliminary framework for a prospective Impact Taxonomy tailored specifically for Swiss fintech enterprises.

3 Theoretical Embedding

The concept of Impact Investing is embedded within the broader framework of sustainable and responsible investing. Within this framework, Impact Investing is defined as the practice of investing in companies, organizations, and funds with the intention of generating a measurable, beneficial social or environmental impact, in addition to a financial return (Dahms et al., 2019, p. 15). Further theoretical foundations are outlined in Chap. 3 Revisiting Theory.

4 Research Question

The primary objective of this research is to establish an initial framework for impact criteria, applicable to Swiss fintech enterprises and to identify the currently prevailing delineation of decision-making processes in evaluating the attained impact. To accomplish this, the research will encompass pivotal sectors such as "Open Finance", "Open Banking", and "Cybersecurity" undertaking an exhaustive examination of the pertinent fintechs within each domain. By engaging in meticulous identification and analysis of these selected fintechs, the research at hand endeavors to contribute to a comprehensive understanding of impact assessment within the Swiss fintech landscape and aims to address the subsequent research questions.

Research Questions

(1) Which determinants should an impact taxonomy for Swiss fintechs contain in order to categorize the generated impact uniformly?
(2) What methods can be used to collect evidence-based impact and ESG data in the fintech industry?

5 Limitations

This study confines its scientific research strictly to the fields of "Open Banking" and "Open Finance" in the fintech industry. Therefore, the research explicitly excluded deposit and lending firms, as well as other subsets of fintech, such as regulatory technology (Regtech) and insurance technology (Insurtech). Moreover, the research is geographically limited to Switzerland, therefore foreign fintechs will be out of scope. The primary basis of this study focused mainly on establishing the general approach Swiss fintechs take in determining the measurement of impact before integrating the learned particulars into standardized impact classification. Accordingly, future research endeavors should strive to delve more profoundly into this subject matter to attain a further comprehensive understanding of the implications and potential outcomes stemming from the findings presented within this study.

Research Methodology

2

In the following chapters, the systematic approach employed to conduct the study is elucidated, ensuring the dependability, accuracy, and applicability of the findings. Furthermore, a thorough presentation of the research design, research approach, pre-interview and main interview participant selection process, and an overview of the interview sample as well as the data-gathering techniques are outlined.

1 Research Design

In the relatively unexplored domain of Impact Investing, particularly regarding such taxonomy, this study endeavors to undertake an exploratory approach. Initially, an examination of the extant body of knowledge within the Impact Investing literature will be conducted, establishing a robust foundation. Subsequently, qualitative interviews will be carried out with representatives of financial technology firms and Impact Investing experts to meticulously scrutinize and analyze their approach for collecting Impact and ESG Data and to determine which criteria should be considered for establishing an impact taxonomy for Swiss fintechs in order to categorize the generated impact in a consistent way. This information will prove indispensable for the formulation of an initial concept for an Impact Investing taxonomy tailored specifically for Swiss fintech firms.

Following the development of the proposed impact taxonomy, a quantitative survey will be employed to evaluate its effectiveness. An in-depth statistical analysis will be subsequently conducted to ascertain the utility of the established criteria. In conclusion, a series of pragmatic recommendations will be provided to facilitate the practical application of the study and furnish a foundation for a potential impact taxonomy.

K. Wendt, M. Hauser, *Green FinTech*, Sustainable Finance,
https://doi.org/10.1007/978-3-031-78279-4_2

2 Research Approach

Due to the fact that observations from qualitative interviews serve as the foundation for the research operations, the research methodology is defined as inductive research. A standardized impact taxonomy for Swiss fintechs is derived from the insights gained from qualitative expert interviews. Therefore, the overall research approach can be determined as a mixed-methods approach since, on the one hand, qualitative interviews and, on the other hand, a quantitative survey will be conducted (Fig. 2.1).

3 Overview Pre-Interview Sample

In order to ensure a standardized methodological approach for defining the interview sample, a pre-interview round was carried out during the preliminary study. The main intention of the pre-interviews was to determine relevant Swiss fintechs with regard to a high-impact generation. Therefore, the approach is defined to find best-in-class Swiss fintechs within each category. Thus, the insights gained from the interviews should have a high informative value. For the pre-interviews, leading Swiss Associations and Venture Capital Funds were contacted due to their valuable expertise within the fintech industry. From a total of eight contacted interview partners, three interview partners (1 Association, 2 Venture Capital Funds) have accepted the interview request, as shown in Table 2.1: Pre-Interview Sample.

4 Interview Sample Methodology

Prior to conducting the qualitative interviews, a preliminary overview of the potential fintechs was developed by a brainstorming session and desk research. Following this, a wide range of significant impact fintechs in Switzerland could be identified through three qualitative interviews, which were later supported by an independent desk study. The entries were then subjected to a qualitative refinement process, wherein businesses that did not align with the criteria for "ESG", "Impact", and "Fintech" as outlined in Sect. 1 in Chap.3 were eliminated. Similarly, fintech enterprises not operating within the defined categories of "Open Banking", "Open Finance", and "Cybersecurity" as well as those not headquartered in Switzerland, were excluded. This rigorous methodology ensured a thorough and comprehensive scientific approach for defining the interview sample. Additionally, the remaining

Fig. 2.1 Research methodology

Table 2.1 Pre-interview sample

Category	Reason for inclusion in the pre-interviews sample
Accepted interview requests:	
Association	Managing partner of an independent private equity firm, university lecturer at top-tier business schools, as well as a member of a leading Swiss Private Equity and Corporate Finance Association
Venture capital fund	Head of Corporate Venture Capital at a leading Swiss financial institution, a Board Observer at various national and international fintechs and startups and both professional and educational international experience at top-tier firms and universities
Venture capital fund	Head of Investor Relations at a leading Swiss Venture Capital firm within the world-renowned Crypto Valley in Zug, besides having experience with the advisory of Ultra-High-Net-Worth Individuals and holds an MBA at one of the most prestigious universities.
Rejected interview requests:	
Association	A Swiss cross-industry initiative that aims to strengthen and anchor Switzerland as a leading global location for digital innovation
Association	Swiss foundation that connects cutting-edge technology with environmental protection for the benefit of people and nature
Venture capital fund	One of the leading Swiss fintech incubators and accelerators
Venture capital fund	An early-stage venture capital investor who focuses on international fintechs developing blockchain solutions
Venture capital fund	A leading Swiss venture capital investor

fintechs were classified according to the ESG methodology of MSCI (2022), as shown in Table 2.2: MSCI ESG methodology template, in order to determine the environmental, social, and governance-related impact of the respective fintechs. Each fintech has been analyzed regarding its impact on the 35 key issues, as outlined by the MSCI's ESG methodology and its underlying rating score composition. It is important to note that certain key issues may not be applicable to some fintechs due to the nature of their business activities within the defined categories. To comprehensively evaluate the impacts, both direct and indirect effects were examined, considering that many fintech firms have a more significant indirect impact than a direct one. The direct impacts on ESG criteria were denoted by "x", while indirect impacts were represented by "(x)" as indicated in Tables 2.3, 2.4, and 2.5.

Step 1: Brainstorming Session & Desk Research

Firstly, potential impact fintechs have been identified through a brainstorming session and an independent desk research, which resulted in the sample according to Table 2.3: Interview Sample Methodology Step 1.

Step 2: Identification of Relevant Impact Fintechs Through Qualitative Interviews

Secondly, the identified fintechs in step 1 have been introduced during the qualitative pre-interviews and supported with several further potential Swiss impact

Table 2.2 MSCI ESG methodology template

ESG rating		Category:	Fintech:
Environmental	*Climate change*	Carbon emissions	Financing environmental impact
		Product carbon footprint	Climate change vulnerability
	Natural capital	Water stress	Biodiversity & land use
		Raw material sourcing	
	Pollution & waste	Toxic emissions & waste	Packaging material & waste
		Electronic waste	
	Environmental opportunities	Opportunities in clean tech	Opportunities in green building
		Opportunities in renewable energy	
Social	*Human capital*	Labor management	Human capital development
		Health & safety	Supply chain labor standards
	Product liability	Product safety & quality	Chemical safety
		Consumer financial protection	Privacy & data security
		Responsible investment	Insuring health & demographic risk
	Stakeholder opposition	Controversial sourcing	Community relations
	Social opportunities	Access to communication	Access to Finance
		Access to health care	Opportunities in nutrition & health
Governance	*Corporate governance*	Ownership & control	Pay
		Board	Accounting
	Corporate behavior	Business ethics	Tax transparency

fintechs, according to the expertise of the expert pre-interview partners. Simultaneously, the identified fintechs have been screened by an independent desk research and those that do not meet the geographical or business model requirements were filtered out.

Step 3: Supplementation by Desk Research

During the last step, further Swiss impact fintechs have been identified through an independent desk research and "sustainable" fintechs from the IFZ Fintech study 2022, according to Ankenbrand (2022), were considered and filtered according to the definitions given above.

Table 2.3 Interview sample methodology Step 1

Company	*Environmental impact*	*Social impact*	*Governance impact*
Open Banking:			
Relai AG	(x)	x	
Cardano Foundation	x	x	x
Tezos Foundation	x	x	x
Mt Pelerin Group AG		x	x
TWINT AG		x	x
Aave Sagl	*Excluded from the sample (Decentralized cryptocurrency lending platform)*		
Open Finance:			
Inyova AG	x	x	(x)
Sygnum Bank AG	x		x
SEBA Bank AG		x	x
neon Switzerland AG	x	x	x
Bitcoin Suisse AG		x	x
Everon AG		x	x
vlot AG	*Excluded from the sample (Category: Insurtech)*		
Cybersecurity:			
Cysec SA		x	
Exeon AG		x	

5 Overview Interview Sample

For the primary interview phase, a diverse sample of best-in-class Swiss fintechs within each category was selected according to the preliminary study. The targeted companies included 26 prominent Swiss fintechs. Despite employing a thorough outreach strategy to ensure a high response rate, no fintech agreed to take part in the survey, resulting in a response rate of 0%, which could indicate that the current state of impact measurement in the fintech sector is limited. Therefore, even best-in-class fintechs seem to have difficulty in consistently and uniformly determining the impact of their business model, or they might not be willing to disclose their approach. Nonetheless, this conclusion might not be entirely valid, since one could assume that if a fintech found a standardized approach to assess its impact, it would most likely actively inform the users and investors of its success.

Since the initially targeted fintech firms did not accept the interview request, the interview sample was enlarged to Swiss fintechs, Impact as well as ESG experts, university professors, and research associates by strategically exploiting personal contacts. Accordingly, the interview sample of Swiss fintechs was extended to a total of 34 fintechs, and a Co-Founder and Head of Investments of a leading Swiss fintech could be attained. In addition, a leading Swiss Impact Investment Manager, two Impact and ESG Specialists from a global specialist in alternative investing, a Co-Founder of a leading Swiss Smart Bank, a university professor serving as the

Table 2.4 Interview sample methodology Step 2

Company	*Environmental impact*	*Social impact*	*Governance impact*
Open Banking:			
Relai AG	(x)	x	
Cardano Foundation	x	x	x
Tezos Foundation	x	x	x
Mt Pelerin Group AG		x	x
TWINT AG		x	x
ecoo AG		x	
PayGreen AG	x	x	
neon Switzerland AG	x	x	x
Klarna Bank AB	*Excluded from the sample (Based outside Switzerland)*		
Moon Pay Limited	*Excluded from the sample (Based outside Switzerland)*		
Revolut Bank UAB	*Excluded from the sample (Based outside Switzerland)*		
SumUp Payments Limited	*Excluded from the sample (Based outside Switzerland)*		
Wise Payments Limited	*Excluded from the sample (Based outside Switzerland)*		
Open Finance:			
Inyova AG	x	x	(x)
Sygnum Bank AG	x		x
SEBA Bank AG		x	x
neon Switzerland AG	x	x	x
Bitcoin Suisse AG		x	x
Everon AG		x	x
Swissquote Bank AG		x	x
SBorg SA (Swissborg)	x	x	x
Impaakt AG	(x)	x	(x)
3rd-eyes analytics AG	(x)	x	
Descartes Finance AG	*Excluded from the sample (Does not qualify as a fintech)*		
Globalance Bank AG	*Excluded from the sample (Does not qualify as a fintech)*		
radicant bank ag	*Excluded from the sample (Does not qualify as a fintech)*		
responsAbility Investments AG	*Excluded from the sample (Does not qualify as a fintech)*		
Whitebox GmbH	*Excluded from the sample (Based outside Switzerland)*		
Cybersecurity:			
Cysec SA		x	
Exeon AG		x	
Futurae Technologies AG		x	
dq technologies AG (Decentriq)		x	
Sinpex GmbH		x	

Head of a Blockchain Center, and three Research Associates specializing in Distributed Ledger Technology (DLT) and fintech-related subjects were contacted as well. The cybersecurity category was excluded because no interviews with fintechs in this arena could be established and due to the realization that the impact

Table 2.5 Interview sample methodology Step 3

Company	*Environmental impact*	*Social impact*	*Governance impact*
Open Banking:			
Relai AG	(x)	x	
Cardano Foundation	x	x	x
Tezos Foundation	x	x	x
Mt Pelerin Group AG		x	x
TWINT AG		x	x
ecoo AG		x	
PayGreen AG	x	x	
neon Switzerland AG	x	x	x
Sonect AG		x	
MyDIO SA		x	
Fea Money Switzerland GmbH		x	
Open Finance:			
Inyova AG	x	x	(x)
Sygnum Bank AG	x		x
SEBA Bank AG		x	x
neon Switzerland AG	x	x	x
Bitcoin Suisse AG		x	x
Everon AG		x	x
Swissquote Bank AG		x	x
SBorg SA (Swissborg)	x	x	x
3rd-eyes analytics AG	(x)	x	
MARK Investment Holding AG (Splint Invest)		x	
Aktionariat AG	*Excluded from the sample (Does not qualify for Open Finance)*		
blueyellow AG	*Excluded from the sample (Does not qualify for Open Finance)*		
Impaakt AG	*Excluded from the sample (Does not qualify for Open Finance)*		
Cybersecurity:			
Cysec SA		x	
Exeon AG		x	
Futurae Technologies AG		x	
dq technologies AG (Decentriq)		x	
Sinpex GmbH		x	

generation differs substantially from the Open Banking and Open Finance category, since the primary objective lies in enhancing security measures.

In order to ensure the preservation of personal anonymity, the authors intentionally abstain from disclosing the additional fintechs and individuals contacted.

6 Quantitative Survey

In this chapter, a comprehensive and in-depth overview of the methodological approach for the quantitative survey is described. It identifies and describes essential parameters: the formulation of the hypothesis, definition of the target group, general survey design, sample size, suitable survey implementation techniques, and data collection. Moreover, ethical considerations, which are filed as part of the data collection stage will be addressed.

The primary objective of the quantitative survey is to discern and analyze the degree of usefulness experienced by Swiss fintechs of the developed Impact Taxonomy. Additionally, the perceived utility of the corresponding Impact Themes, Impact Factors, and Key Performance Indicators (KPIs) within the Impact Taxonomy is assessed. This survey will assist in identifying specific areas of these components to be further optimized, which could ultimately enhance the effectiveness and applicability of the Impact Taxonomy. Furthermore, this survey will facilitate the identification of elements that could potentially be omitted from the final version of the Impact Taxonomy.

6.1 Hypothesis Development

In accordance with the methodological framework delineated in Fig. 2.2 of Sect. 2 research, the development of the Impact Taxonomy was deemed essential as a preliminary step for the accurate formulation of specific hypotheses pertinent to the data analysis phase. Consequently, following the identification of Impact Themes, Strategic Goals and KPIs for the Bottom-up approach, encompassing Open Banking and Open Finance, as well as the identification of Impact Factors, Strategic Objectives, and Performance Metrics for the top-down approach, the corresponding hypotheses were systematically established (Tables 2.6 and 2.7).

Hypotheses for the Bottom-up Approach (Open Banking / Open Finance)

Hypotheses for the top-down approach

6.2 Determination of the Target Group

For the distribution of the quantitative survey, a meticulous approach was taken in selecting the target group to ensure a broad-based, balanced, and representative sample was reached. The sample was chosen from the best-in-class impact fintechs identified through the preliminary study sampling approach. These best-in-class impact fintechs were mainly selected due to their excellence in embedding impact-driven practices in their operations. In order to capture a broader range of perspectives, the sample was expanded by including fintechs identified in the IFZ fintech Study 2023 (Ankenbrand et al., 2023). In fact, this study is well established in the

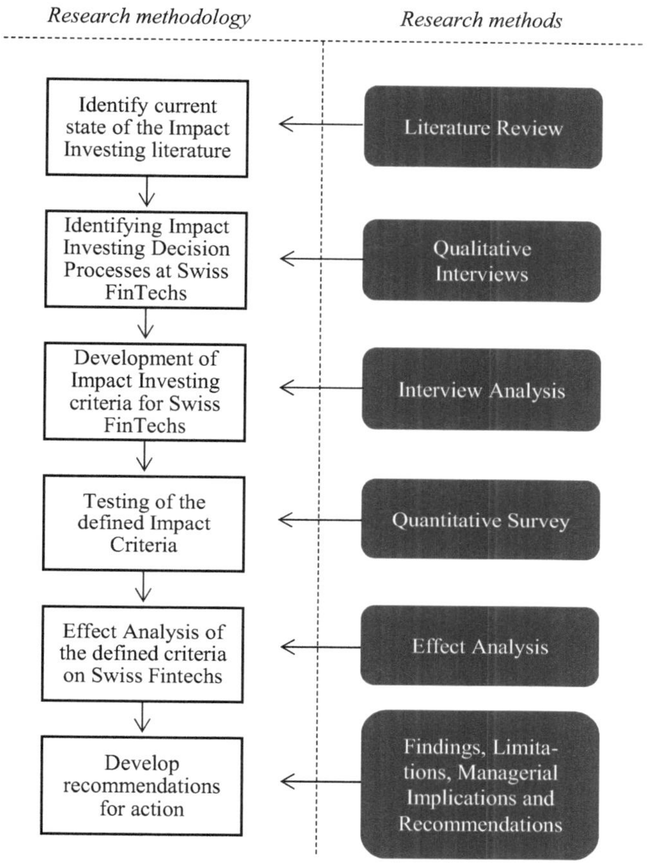

Fig. 2.2 Inductive resonant research approach. Source: Adapted graphic based on Streefkerk (2019)

Swiss fintech industry and has therefore provided valuable insights due to its deep analysis of the Swiss fintech landscape. Consequently, the survey sample has been enriched by including the best-in-class impact fintechs and fintechs identified in the IFZ fintech Study 2023, further ensuring a cross-sectional overview of the industry. By employing this technique, overall validity and generalizability of the findings improved because it became possible to collect heterogeneous opinions and diverse practices within the Swiss fintech industry to provide a holistic view of the industry.

6.3 Sample Size

With regard to the sample size, the overall boundaries of the Swiss fintech landscape were apparent. The objective of the study was to include a broad spectrum of Swiss fintechs with a clear priority on best-in-class fintechs that had made significant

Table 2.6 Hypotheses bottom-up approach Open Banking and Open Finance

Financial inclusion:		
1	H_0:	Open Banking and Open Finance fintechs have the same expected scoring values for the "Financial inclusion" dimension and are therefore considered homogeneous in their sustainability preferences.
2	H_A:	Open Banking and Open Finance fintechs do not have the same expected scoring values according to the "Financial inclusion" dimension and are therefore considered to be heterogeneous in their sustainability preferences.
Financial literacy:		
3	H_0:	Open Banking and Open Finance fintechs have the same expected scoring values for the "Financial literacy" dimension and are therefore considered homogeneous in their sustainability preferences.
4	H_A:	Open Banking and Open Finance fintechs do not have the same expected scoring values according to the "Financial literacy" dimension and are therefore considered to be heterogeneous in their sustainability preferences.
Transparency:		
5	H_0:	Open Banking and Open Finance fintechs have the same expected scoring values for the "Transparency" dimension and are therefore considered homogeneous in their sustainability preferences.
6	H_A:	Open Banking and Open Finance fintechs do not have the same expected scoring values according to the "Transparency" dimension and are therefore considered to be heterogeneous in their sustainability preferences.
Affordability:		
7	H_0:	Open Banking and Open Finance fintechs have the same expected scoring values for the "Affordability" dimension and are therefore considered homogeneous in their sustainability preferences.
8	H_A:	Open Banking and Open Finance fintechs do not have the same expected scoring values according to the "Affordability" dimension and are therefore considered to be heterogeneous in their sustainability preferences.
Efficiency:		
9	H_0:	Open Banking and Open Finance fintechs have the same expected scoring values for the "Efficiency" dimension and are therefore considered homogeneous in their sustainability preferences.
10	H_A:	Open Banking and Open Finance fintechs do not have the same expected scoring values according to the "Efficiency" dimension and are therefore considered to be heterogeneous in their sustainability preferences.
Personalization:		
11	H_0:	Open Banking and Open Finance fintechs have the same expected scoring values for the "Personalization" dimension and are therefore considered homogeneous in their sustainability preferences.

(continued)

Table 2.6 (continued)

12	H_A:	Open Banking and Open Finance fintechs do not have the same expected scoring values according to the "Personalization" dimension and are therefore considered to be heterogeneous in their sustainability preferences.
Security:		
13	H_0:	Open Banking and Open Finance fintechs have the same expected scoring values for the "Security" dimension and are therefore considered homogeneous in their sustainability preferences.
14	H_A:	Open Banking and Open Finance fintechs do not have the same expected scoring values according to the "Security" dimension and are therefore considered to be heterogeneous in their sustainability preferences.
Economic growth:		
15	H_0:	Open Banking and Open Finance fintechs have the same expected scoring values for the "Economic growth" dimension and are therefore considered homogeneous in their sustainability preferences.
16	H_A:	Open Banking and Open Finance fintechs do not have the same expected scoring values according to the "Economic growth" dimension and are therefore considered to be heterogeneous in their sustainability preferences.
Personalization:		
17	H_0:	Open Banking and Open Finance fintechs have the same expected scoring values for the "Personalization" dimension and are therefore considered homogeneous in their sustainability preferences.
18	H_A:	Open Banking and Open Finance fintechs do not have the same expected scoring values according to the "Personalization" dimension and are therefore considered to be heterogeneous in their sustainability preferences.
Sustainability:		
19	H_0:	Open Banking and Open Finance fintechs have the same expected scoring values for the "Sustainability" dimension and are therefore considered homogeneous in their sustainability preferences.
20	H_A:	Open Banking and Open Finance fintechs do not have the same expected scoring values according to the "Sustainability" dimension and are therefore considered to be heterogeneous in their sustainability preferences.
Innovation:		
21	H_0:	Open Banking and Open Finance fintechs have the same expected scoring values for the "Innovation" dimension and are therefore considered homogeneous in their sustainability preferences.
22	H_A:	Open Banking and Open Finance fintechs do not have the same expected scoring values according to the "Innovation" dimension and are therefore considered to be heterogeneous in their sustainability preferences.
Gender equality:		
23	H_0:	Open Banking and Open Finance fintechs have the same expected scoring values for the "Gender equality" dimension and are therefore considered homogeneous in their sustainability preferences.

(continued)

Table 2.6 (continued)

24	H_A:	Open Banking and Open Finance fintechs do not have the same expected scoring values according to the "Gender equality" dimension and are therefore considered to be heterogeneous in their sustainability preferences.
Financial resilience:		
25	H_0:	Open Banking and Open Finance fintechs have the same expected scoring values for the "Financial resilience" dimension and are therefore considered homogeneous in their sustainability preferences.
26	H_A:	Open Banking and Open Finance fintechs do not have the same expected scoring values according to the "Financial resilience" dimension and are therefore considered to be heterogeneous in their sustainability preferences.

contributions to the industry. A sampling strategy was put in place with the effort to ensure the utmost level of conformity with the underlying geographical location of the fintechs. Therefore, in order to account for the fact that a significant number of Swiss fintechs are headquartered in either Zurich or Zug, the sample was chosen to accurately reflect this distribution.

6.4 Design of the Survey

A quantitative online survey has been employed as the instrumental tool for conducting the empirical study. The survey participants are provided with a set of response options on a 5-point Likert scale, as outlined in Table 2.8, to assess the designated Impact Themes, Strategic Objectives, and Key Performance Indicators (KPIs) encompassed within the Impact Taxonomy.

In order to categorize the types of sustainability preferences based on the online survey responses, the response options are each assigned to specific scoring values. The Likert scale, ranging from one to five, is transformed into a scoring range of zero to ten, where higher values indicate a greater preference for the respective Impact Theme, Strategic Objective, or Key Performance Indicator (KPI). This approach was employed to enhance the comparability of the scoring values. Thus, the standardized response options are allocated the following scoring values (Table 2.9):

The quantitative survey has been uniformly composed in the English language, taking into consideration the anticipated prevalence of English as the primary means of communication at the majority of Swiss fintechs.

6.5 Survey Technique and Data Collection

In order to obtain further information about the participants and possible significant correlations between segments, socio-demographic data is collected at the beginning of the survey. The following socio-demographic data is collected (Table 2.10).

Table 2.7 Hypotheses top-down approach Open Banking and Open Finance

Environmental factors:		
27	H_0:	Open Banking and Open Finance fintechs have the same expected scoring values for the "Environmental factors" dimension and are therefore considered homogeneous in their sustainability preferences.
28	H_A:	Open Banking and Open Finance fintechs do not have the same expected scoring values according to the "Environmental factors" dimension and are therefore considered to be heterogeneous in their sustainability preferences.
Social factors:		
29	H_0:	Open Banking and Open Finance fintechs have the same expected scoring values for the "Social factors" dimension and are therefore considered homogeneous in their sustainability preferences.
30	H_A:	Open Banking and Open Finance fintechs do not have the same expected scoring values according to the "Social factors" dimension and are therefore considered to be heterogeneous in their sustainability preferences.
Governance factors:		
31	H_0:	Open Banking and Open Finance fintechs have the same expected scoring values for the "Governance factors" dimension and are therefore considered homogeneous in their sustainability preferences.
32	H_A:	Open Banking and Open Finance fintechs do not have the same expected scoring values according to the "Governance factors" dimension and are therefore considered to be heterogeneous in their sustainability preferences.
Economic factors:		
33	H_0:	Open Banking and Open Finance fintechs have the same expected scoring values for the "Economic factors" dimension and are therefore considered homogeneous in their sustainability preferences.
34	H_A:	Open Banking and Open Finance fintechs do not have the same expected scoring values according to the "Economic factors" dimension and are therefore considered to be heterogeneous in their sustainability preferences.
Technological factors:		
35	H_0:	Open Banking and Open Finance fintechs have the same expected scoring values for the "Technological factors" dimension and are therefore considered homogeneous in their sustainability preferences.
36	H_A:	Open Banking and Open Finance fintechs do not have the same expected scoring values according to the "Technological factors" dimension and are therefore considered to be heterogeneous in their sustainability preferences.
Regulatory factors:		
37	H_0:	Open Banking and Open Finance fintechs have the same expected scoring values for the "Regulatory factors" dimension and are therefore considered homogeneous in their sustainability preferences.
38	H_A:	Open Banking and Open Finance fintechs do not have the same expected scoring values according to the "Regulatory factors" dimension and are therefore considered to be heterogeneous in their sustainability preferences.
Integration and Collaboration factors:		
39	H_0:	Open Banking and Open Finance fintechs have the same expected scoring values for the "Integration and Collaboration factors" dimension and are therefore considered homogeneous in their sustainability preferences.
40	H_A:	Open Banking and Open Finance fintechs do not have the same expected scoring values according to the "Integration and Collaboration factors" dimension and are therefore considered to be heterogeneous in their sustainability preferences.

Table 2.8 Quantitative survey answer options

Expression of the answer options				
Highly irrelevant	Irrelevant	Somewhat relevant	Relevant	Highly relevant

Table 2.9 Quantitative survey transformation of survey values to scoring values

	Expression of the answer options				
Answer options	Highly irrelevant	Irrelevant	Somewhat relevant	Relevant	Highly relevant
Survey value	1	2	3	4	5
Scoring value	0	2.5	5	7.5	10

6.6 Ethics

In developing the research design and carrying out the empirical study, it's imperative to address any ethical concerns that may arise with regard to the data collection process. Due to the fact that the study involves the collection of data from individuals, safeguarding personal privacy is of paramount importance. Consequently, before administering the online survey questionnaire, the respondents were informed about the research context and purpose. They were also informed about the method of data storage and processing, the guarantees of anonymity, and the rights to which they were entitled. Participation in the survey was considered valid only after personal data processing was accepted electronically.

6.7 Data Processing

The collected data was processed in a manner that facilitated both descriptive and inferential data analyses. To elucidate the underlying causes of the identified preferences for the categories within the Impact Taxonomy using socio-demographic data, dependency analyses were conducted in the form of multiple regression models. Statistical data processing was carried out with the assistance of analytical software programs, such as Microsoft Excel and IBM SPSS Statistics.

Table 2.10 Sociodemographic survey data

Sociodemographic data	Fine characteristics
Role	Chief Executive Officer (CEO) Founder / Co-Founder Chief Financial Officer (CFO) Chief Operating Officer (COO) Chief Technology Officer (CTO) Chief Marketing Officer (CMO) Chief Compliance Officer (CCO) Chief Risk Officer (CRO) Chief Investment Officer (CIO) Other
Swiss Canton	Aargau Appenzell Ausserrhoden Appenzell Innerrhoden Basel-Landschaft Basel-Stadt Bern Freiburg Genève (Geneva) Glarus Graubünden (Grisons) Jura Lucerne Neuchâtel Nidwalden Obwalden St. Gallen Schaffhausen Schwyz Solothurn Thurgau Ticino Uri Vaud Valais (Wallis) Zug Zurich
Gender	male female diverse
Age	18–29 years 30–39 years 40–49 years 50–65 years > 65 years

(continued)

Table 2.10 (continued)

Sociodemographic data	Fine characteristics
Sustainability-related groups	American Investment Capital (AIC)—Guidelines for Responsible Investing American Sustainable Business Network (merger of American Sustainable Business Council and Social Venture Circle) Asian Venture Philanthropy Network (AVPN) Aspen Network of Development Entrepreneurs (ANDE) Black Philanthropic Network (BPN) Ceres Certified B Corporations Climate Action 100+ ESG Data Convergence Project European Venture Philanthropy Association (EVPA) Global Impact Investing Network (GIIN) Global Real Estate Sustainability Benchmark (GRESB) Global Reporting Initiative (GRI) Global Steering Group (GSG) for Impact Investment IFRS Sustainability Disclosure Standards (the foundation of which was SASB) ImpactAssets (IA 50) Impact Management Norms (Impact Frontiers) Institutional Limited Partners Association (ILPA) ESG Policies and Reporting Intergovernmental Panel on Climate Change (IPCC) International Finance Corporation (IFC) Mission Investors Exchange (MIE) Principles for Responsible Investment (PRI) Sustainable Finance Disclosure Regulation (SFDR) Task Force on Climate-related Financial Disclosures (TCFD) Triple Bottom Line Investing (TBLI) UN Sustainable Development Goals (SDGs) US SIF (Forum for Sustainable and Responsible Investment) VentureESG None Other

3 Revisiting Theory of Sustainable Investing: ESG and Impact

Primarily, a paramount comprehension of the pertinent terminology, namely "ESG", "Impact" and "Fintech" is established as a foundational prerequisite for delineating the interview sample. Subsequently, an exhaustive literature review is conducted to present the current state of research and expound upon the prevailing developments. Additionally, an encompassing portrayal of the impact investment landscape is provided, while pertinent reporting standards are introduced for comprehensive understanding.

1 Definition of Terms

In this chapter, the relevant terms used to determine the qualitative interview sample are defined. Therefore, the following definitions will lead to exclusions from the interview sample in case the outlined definition is not met by Swiss fintechs.

1.1 Definition ESG

The origins of sustainable development go back to the formation of sustainable forestry by Hans Carl von Carlowitz (1645–1714), who called for sustainable use of the forest so that long-term economic benefit of the forest can be ensured (Gottschlich & Friedrich, 2014, pp. 23–29). Later on, within the Brundtland Report by the United Nations (1987), the term sustainable development has been described as "*Humanity has the ability to make development sustainable to ensure that it meets the needs of the present without compromising the ability of future generations to meet their own needs.*" (p. 15). Over the past decades, non-financial information has become increasingly in demand. This type of data was utilized for socially responsible investing (SRI) initiatives as early as the 1960s, contradicting the conventional capital market view, which considers that a company's responsibility lies solely with its

K. Wendt, M. Hauser, *Green FinTech*, Sustainable Finance,
https://doi.org/10.1007/978-3-031-78279-4_3

shareholders. Environmental, Social, and Governance (ESG) concerns and the risks they pose have lately gained financial value in the eyes of the investing community. There has been an increase in interest in ESG data as a result of investors' attention shifting from values-driven Socially Responsible Investing (SRI) to financial value-driven ESG (Eccles et al., 2020, p. 575). ESG mainly refers to criteria for presenting and evaluating the sustainability of business activities, particularly in the case of financial investments. These sustainability criteria are broken down into the areas of the Environment "E", Social "S", and responsible Corporate Governance "G" (Erchinger, 2022, p. 8). Therefore, the authors relate to the definition of the term mentioned above when discussing ESG in subsequent chapters.

1.2 Definition Impact

According to Bugg-Levine and Emerson (2011), the term Impact Investing originated at a meeting amongst a group of 20 investors and industry pioneers at the Rockefeller Foundation in 2007 (p. 12). Impact Investing can be defined by four distinct categories, which are undertaken by many investors in the sequence shown in Fig. 3.1: Impact Investing Path. This path starts with responsible investment (exclusion lists, best-in-class selection for the remaining assets), sustainable investment (according to ESG criteria), thematic investment and lastly ends up at impact first investments (Wendt, 2018, p. 7). According to the Global Impact Investing Network "*Impact investments are investments made with the intention to generate positive, measurable social and environmental impact alongside a financial return.*" (Global Impact Investing Network, 2020). Therefore, it can be noted that one of the core drivers of an impact investor is to generate not only positive financial returns but also quantifiable positive social or environmental returns. The authors refer to the definition of the Global Impact Investing Network when referring to impact investments in later chapters.

1.3 Definition Fintech

In recent years, fintech solutions have become increasingly popular and are tapping into the traditional banking customer segment. In order to fully determine the range of possible software offerings, it is crucial to understand various terminology definitions. Langley and Leyshon (2021) define the term as "*FinTech is the recognised descriptor for an emergent and diverse sector of digital retail monetary and financial services.*" (p. 376). According to Dorfleitner et al. (2017), fintechs "... *combine*

Fig. 3.1 Impact Investing Path. Source: Adapted graphic based on Wendt (2018)

financial services with modern, innovative technologies. As a rule, new participants in the market offer Internet-based and application-oriented products. FinTechs generally aim to attract customers with products and services that are more user-friendly, efficient, transparent, and automated than those currently available." (p. 5). Whereas Ankenbrand (2022) offers a broader definition and explains the term in more detail: *"FinTech is defined as technology-based solutions for innovative products, services, and processes in the financial industry, improving, complementing, and/or disrupting existing offerings. Hence, FinTech companies are firms whose main activities, core competencies, and/or strategic focus lie in developing those solutions."* (p. 3). Consequently, when referring to fintechs in subsequent chapters, the authors refer to the definition of the term according to Ankenbrand (2022).

1.4 GHG Protocol Scopes and Emissions

GHG Protocol is a standardized way of measuring and reporting greenhouse gas emissions. It consists of three scopes defining several emissions sources to be considered for calculating emissions, as shown in Fig. 3.2: Scopes and Emissions. Emissions from sources owned or controlled by an organization are recognized as Scope 1 emissions. For instance, Scope 1 emissions would constitute waste generated within the organization's boundaries, refrigerant leaks, or combustion emissions from burning fuels. Scope 2 emissions are indirect but inevitable by-products of creating the organization's purchased electricity, steam, heating, and cooling systems. As the organization does not have direct control over the components' production, the emissions from the production of Scope 2 fuels are often regarded as "market-based" emissions. Scope 3 emissions are all other additional indirect

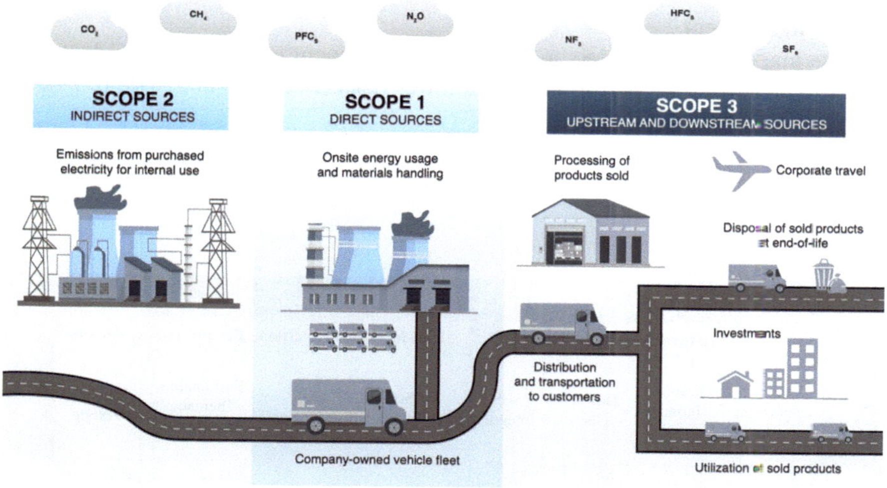

Fig. 3.2 Scopes and emissions. Source: Adapted graphic based on Oliver Wyman Forum, 2021

emissions associated with the operation of the organization but not included in Scope 2. Some examples of Scope three emissions include: emissions from garbage disposal, business travel, and usage of sold goods (Greenhouse Gas Protocol, 2013).

2 Sustainable Investment Landscape

In the forthcoming chapters, a comprehensive depiction of the prevailing investment approaches will be presented, and an extensive enumeration of the multitudinous investment methodologies will be delineated.

2.1 Sustainable Investment Strategies

According to Dahms et al. (2019), the overall sustainable investment landscape can be categorized by eight investment approaches, which mainly differ in their focus on either traditional investing, sustainable investment approaches, or philanthropy, as shown in Fig. 3.3: Sustainable Investment Strategies. On the one hand, traditional investing is categorized by no systematic consideration of ESG and impact aspects. On the other hand, sustainable investment approaches consist of multiple different strategies, which distinguish in terms of the pre- or post-investment decision horizon (pp. 14–15). The different strategies are described in further detail below.

Best-in-Class

An approach using a sustainability rating to evaluate an issuer's or company's ESG performance against that of its competitors. All organizations or issuers with ratings above a specified level are considered to be investable (Dahms et al., 2019, p. 14).

ESG Engagement

Efforts made by shareholders to persuade management to consider ESG factors in order to enhance ESG performance and lower risks (Dahms et al., 2019, p. 14).

<table>
<tr><td rowspan="3">Traditional Investing</td><td colspan="8">Sustainable Investment Approaches</td><td rowspan="3">Philanthropy</td></tr>
<tr><td colspan="4">Pre-investment decision</td><td colspan="2">Post-investment decision</td><td colspan="2">Pre-investment decision</td></tr>
<tr><td>Exclusions</td><td>Norms-based Screening</td><td>Best-in-Class</td><td>ESG Integration</td><td>ESG Voting</td><td>ESG Engagement</td><td>Sustainable Thematic Investments</td><td>Impact Investing</td></tr>
</table>

Fig. 3.3 Sustainable investment strategies. Source: Adapted graphic based on Dahms et al., 2019, p. 15

ESG Integration
The explicit incorporation of ESG opportunities and risks by investors into conventional financial analysis and investment choices based on a structured methodology and reliable research sources (Dahms et al., 2019, p. 14).

ESG Voting
An approach when investors actively utilize their voting rights to address issues concerning ESG criteria or ESG policies (Dahms et al., 2019, p. 14).

Exclusions
A strategy that excludes organizations, nations, or other issuers based on actions deemed unsuitable for investment. Exclusion criteria may include activities, product categories, or corporate policies (Dahms et al., 2019, p. 14).

Impact Investing
Investments designed to produce a financial return as well as a demonstrable, positive social and environmental effect. Depending on the situation, impact investments can be done in both developing and mature economies and aim for a range of returns from below-market to above-market rates. (Dahms et al., 2019, p. 14).

Norms-Based Screening
This approach aims at investment screening against minimal norms of business behavior based on national or international standards (Dahms et al., 2019, p. 14).

Sustainable Thematic Investments
Investing in companies that provide sustainable solutions for environmental or social issues (Dahms et al., 2019, p. 14).

2.2 Impact Investing Market Volume

The Impact Investing industry marks its origin in 2007 and has experienced rapid growth ever since. Over half of active Impact Investing organizations were founded within the past decade. As of the end of 2018, it is projected that the value of Assets under Management (AuM) was around $502 billion. However, the size of individual investor portfolios differs significantly. While the median AuM for investors was $29 million, the average was $452 million. This implies that although most organizations are of relatively modest sizes, a few investors manage considerably significant Impact Investing portfolios. Furthermore, asset managers account for about half of the projected AuM, which reflects the fact that many impact investors prefer to direct cash through specialist managers, which include managers in public equity, real estate, fixed income, venture capital, and private equity managers. The industry is expanding to address critical global challenges for the planet, and there is optimism as $13 trillion of professionally managed assets now prioritize sustainability.

This reflects a larger shift in the financial markets towards investments that generate positive social and environmental impact (Mudaliar & Dithrich, 2019, pp. 3–11).

3 Reporting Standards

As mentioned in Sect. 1.2 Definition Impact, the term Impact Investing originated from a meeting at the Rockefeller Foundation in 2007, during which two complementary tools were developed. Firstly, the Impact Reporting and Investment Standards (IRIS) was constructed to provide a standardized toolset for environmental, social, and financial performance. The primary advantages of the reporting standard are enhanced transparency, enhanced ESG factor credibility, and increased corporate comparability (GIIN, 2011, p. 7). Secondly, the Global Impact Investing Ratings System (GIIRS) has been established to offer criteria and a rating system for businesses, investors, and intermediaries (Clarkin & Cangioni, 2016, p. 139). The following chapters will cover these reporting standards in more detail.

3.1 Impact Reporting and Investment Standards (IRIS+)

According to the Global Impact Investing Network (GIIN), impact measurement and management (IMM) are considered one of the critical factors of Impact Investing. GIIN envisions a world where social and environmental considerations are automatically incorporated into investment choices as the standard approach. By establishing and increasing the bar for investment practices and developing the tools and data that enable investors to assess the impact and direct financial resources to the most efficient solutions, Impact Investing may play a crucial part in achieving this objective. Furthermore, IRIS+ makes it simpler for investors to turn their intentions for having a positive impact into actual impact results. Decisions on impact investments must be based on reliable, comparable impact data. Therefore, investors must effectively manage and monitor impact data to determine whether they have the desired impact. In this regard, IRIS+ offers assistance to investors throughout the IMM procedure with the standardized IRIS+ system, which facilitates investors to assess and characterize impact performance by using the IRIS+ core metrics sets as well as the catalogue of metrics (Global Impact Investing Network, 2019, p. 2).

Five Dimensions of Impact
GIIN has established the Impact Management Project (IMP), which is a platform for achieving universal agreement on how to assess and control impact. The IMP discovered that gathering data across five dimensions of impact is necessary to determine impact performance in coordination with the input of over a thousand industry stakeholders (Global Impact Investing Network, 2019, pp. 2–9) (Table 3.1).

Table 3.1 GIIN Dimensions of impact

Dimension of Impact	Description
What is the goal?	Recognizing how the business contributes to the outcomes and how significant the outcomes are to stakeholders
Who is affected?	Recognizing which stakeholders are being impacted and the extent to which they were underserved before the firm's impact
How much change is happening?	Identifying the number of stakeholders who experienced the outcome, the degree of change they observed, and the duration of that experience
What is the contribution?	Determining whether an investor's or an enterprise's efforts led to results that were likely better than what would have occurred in the absence of those efforts
What is the impact risk?	Determining the risk that an impact will differ from what is anticipated

Source: Adapted graphic based on Global Impact Investing Network, 2019

IRIS+ Thematic Taxonomy

Impact investors have been inhibited from sharing and comparing impact performance because of inadequately harmonized definitions of common terminology and Impact Investing topics. To create a consistent terminology for describing, evaluating, communicating, and eventually comparing impact performance, the IRIS+ thematic taxonomy provides widely recognized definitions of Impact Categories and Impact Themes and establishes common goals and Core Metrics Sets per topic. The social and environmental Impact Themes that impact investors (and the businesses or projects in which they invest) use to frame their strategic objectives, portfolios, and business models are used to structure IRIS+. Several existing principles and initiatives were utilized and built upon, such as the Global Reporting Initiative (GRI), the Principles for Responsible Investment (PRI), the Organization for Economic Cooperation and Development (OECD), the United Nations Environment Programme Finance Initiative (UNEP FI), the International Finance Corporation (IFC), Toniic, the Social Performance Task Force (SPTF), the Global Off-Grid Solar Energy Association (GOGLA), and the Food and Agriculture Organization of the United Nations (FAO). Furthermore, the IRIS metrics and thematic taxonomy align with the SDGs and their targets. Besides that, every Impact Category has the potential to have beneficial social or environmental consequences. However, no Impact Category is immune to potential negative implications (McCarthy et al., 2022, pp. 3–4).

In order to transform intentions into quantifiable data and results, the thematic taxonomy uses a hierarchy of classifications that progresses from broad to narrow and begins with the high-level Impact Category (Figs. 3.4 and 3.5). Each impact category contains more detailed Impact Themes, as shown in Fig. 3.6, and illustrative Impact Delivery Models to identify how investors and businesses contribute to impact within any category. Lastly, the taxonomy consists of standard and unique Strategic Goals for which IRIS+ contains evidence-based Core Metrics Sets according to best practices (McCarthy et al., 2022, p. 4). For instance, the development of large-scale wind energy in a developing market could reduce CO_2 emissions (positive environmental impact), increase the availability of electricity for low-income

Fig. 3.4 IRIS+ classification hierarchy. Source: Adapted graphic based on McCarthy et al., 2022

Fig. 3.5 IRIS+ approach to connect an investor's impact goals to an SDG target. Source: Adapted graphic based on Global Impact Investing Network, 2022, p. 5

Impact category	Impact Theme	Impact category	Impact Theme
Agriculture	Food Security	***Land***	Natural Resources Conservation
	Smallholder Agriculture		Sustainable Land Management
	Sustainable Agriculture		Sustainable Forestry
Energy	Clean Energy	***Health***	Access to Quality Health Care
	Energy Access		Nutrition
	Energy Efficiency		
Climate	Climate Change Mitigation	***Diversity & Inclusion***	Gender Lens
	Climate Resilience and Adaptation		Racial Equity
Water	Sustainable Water Management	***Real Estate***	Affordable Quality Housing
	Water, Sanitation, and Hygiene (WASH)		Green Buildings
Oceans and Coastal Zones	Marine Resources Conservation & Management	***Air***	Clean Air
Biodiversity & Ecosystems	Biodiversity & Ecosystem Conservation	***Employment***	Quality Jobs
Education	Access to Quality Education	***Financial Services***	Financial Inclusion
Infrastructure	Resilient Infrastructure	***Pollution***	Pollution Prevention
Waste	Waste Management		

Fig. 3.6 IRIS+ Impact Themes. Source: Adapted graphic based on McCarthy et al., 2022, p. 6

families (positive social impact), and enhance the number of employment opportunities (positive social impact). Nevertheless, it could also have unfavorable effects, such as noise pollution for surrounding communities, birdlife risks, and land management difficulties. Although, IRIS+ does not specify whether specific categories or themes have a higher or lower effect on positive or negative impacts (McCarthy et al., 2022, p. 4). The IRIS+ Catalog of Measures has been assessed against all 169

SDG targets and overall 78 SDGs are compatible with IRIS+. As shown in Fig. 3.5, an investor might define a self-articulated goal, for example, "Increase energy efficiency globally" and align it with the respective target (SDG 7.3: By 2030, double the global rate of improvement in energy efficiency). Based on the selection process of determining the suitable SDG, the investor would screen the IRIS+ Impact Theme Catalog and select "Energy Efficiency" as the appropriate theme. According to the Catalog of Metrics a total of 48 metrics for SDG 7.3 can be identified, and the investor can choose the relevant metrics for the respective investment activities.

IRIS+ Impact Themes

3.2 Global Impact Investing Ratings System (GIIRS) / B Impact Assessment

The Global Impact Investing Rating System is an approach to provide investors with the performance of investment funds and their impacts. The components of the GIIRS assessment are ESG performance, financial performance, and alignment of investments with the stated impact objectives of a given fund, amongst other factors. It is an approach that integrates data about the fund from the internal data repository with data collected from external sources. This data is then agglomerated into the fund's final score, as well as translated into the GIIRS rating on a five-point scale, where one is the lowest and five is the highest possible score. The GIIRS rating system aims to provide an all-encompassing, transparent view to investors regarding the performance and impact of the fund to make better educated investment decisions. Being the case, it also endeavors to help fund managers by adding value to their full performance through advice on how to raise their ratings. In essence, it's a helpful resource for fund managers and investors who want to maximize the impact of their investments (GIIRS, 2012). According to B Lab, the organization behind the GIIRS, it appears that the current GIIRS has been terminated (B Lab Global, 2023). However, B Lab developed a new impact assessment method, the so-called B Impact Assessment (BIA), which is a digital tool used by over 150,000 businesses to measure, manage, and improve their impact. With benchmarking across six impact areas—governance, workers, community, environment, customers, and a disclosure questionnaire—businesses can pinpoint their improvement areas. A verified score of 80 points or more is required to obtain the B Corp Certification. The platform also supports tools and resources for continuous improvement initiatives (B Lab, 2024).

4 General Impact Assessment Methods

The following chapters will examine the nuances of Environmental Impact Assessment (EIA) and Strategic Environmental Assessment (SEA), two critical procedures for assessing and minimizing the environmental effects of proposed projects and strategic decisions.

4.1 Environmental Impact Assessment

Environmental Impact Assessment (EIA) is a method for assisting with decisions and identifying the potential environmental impacts of a proposed project and was first put into place in the USA in 1969 and is now governed by legislation in most nations on earth (Morgan, 2012, pp. 5–6). In light of the necessity for decision-makers to possess knowledge regarding the environmental consequences of their decisions prior to granting approval, the EIA process became closely associated with the concept of sustainable development during the Rio Earth Summit (United Nations Conference on Environment and Development, 1992). The European Union's environmental policy uses a wide variety of tools. For instance, the European Union has created a combination of obligatory and optional processes to evaluate environmental concerns, which are stated under the EU's EIA Directive 2014/52/EU. For a number of different projects, an EIA is required, such as for motorways, express roads, nuclear power stations, long-distance railways, dams of a certain capacity, and waste disposal installations for hazardous waste (European Parliament and the Council of the European Union, 2014). Since the 1970s, various EIA-related forms have emerged, such as the Social Impact Assessment (SIA), Health Impact Assessment (HIA), and SEA. Each method has been developed due to some discontent with EIA as it has been implemented (Morgan, 2012, pp. 6–7).

4.2 Strategic Environmental Assessment

SEA is a methodical, proactive approach to enhancing the significance of environmental concerns in strategic decision-making (Verheem & Tonk, 2000, p. 177). According to Morgan (2012), SEA mainly consists of five relevant steps: screening, scoping, impact prediction, significance, and monitoring as well as other aspects of following-up (p. 9). However, SEA is characterized by a variety of different approaches, which result from the particular settings in which SEA procedures are intended to be applied. Therefore, a worldwide standardized set of principles is yet to be defined (Verheem & Tonk, 2000, pp. 177–178).

5 Impact Creation of Fintechs

The following chapters will delve into the multifaceted manners in which financial technology can contribute to sustainable development. This investigation will cover a wide range of social and environmental issues while highlighting the importance of the generated impact. As a result, emphasis will be put on how important financial technology companies are to creating meaningful change and supporting lasting transitions.

5.1 Impact of Fintechs on Traditional Banking

Swiss fintechs are recognized as pioneers in digital innovation and crucial service providers for Swiss banks. The enhancement of traditional Swiss banks' operational processes, facilitated by collaboration with fintechs, contributes to increased productivity. According to Ankenbrand et al. (2023), the balance sheet total and commission income investment and therefore the total investment rose from 2016 onwards. Swiss banks were able to reduce relative labor costs by 23% by the end of 2021, while general and administrative costs increased to 151% by the same year. Furthermore, the temporal progression of interest and commission income from securities and investment businesses, along with the aggregated total income, peaked at 114% by the end of 2021. In summation, it can be stated that Swiss banking institutions persist in enhancing their efficiency, while costs remain stable in the face of expanding volumes. Although, Swiss banks were most certainly able to benefit from the rise in asset prices in 2021 without having to increase their costs to match (pp. 85–86).

5.2 Financial Inclusion Through Fintechs

Promoting financial inclusion represents one of the most fundamental ways fintechs can generate a positive impact. In numerous developing nations, access to formal financial services remains restricted for a considerable portion of the population (Demirgüç-Kunt et al., 2018, p. 4). According to Demir et al. (2022), who analyzed the interconnection between fintechs, income inequality, and financial inclusion in 140 countries using data from a Global Findex survey in 2011, 2014, and 2017, fintechs impact inequality directly and indirectly through financial inclusion. The study results indicate that financial inclusion is a crucial factor in reducing income inequality through fintechs, but the effects are primarily observed in higher-income countries (p. 86). The primary cause for the limited availability of financial services in developing countries can be attributed to insufficient accessibility or an inadequate credit history. This issue is further compounded by the difficulties individuals face in establishing a formal identity. Consequently, financial institutions perceive these customers as high-risk, thereby elevating the costs associated with conventional banking services to an extent that renders them unattainable for the aforementioned demographic (Blakstad, 2018, p. 12). Furthermore, fintechs have the capacity to bolster financial inclusion by fostering digitization. In delivering financial services, the embracement of digital transformation can lower the cost of operation of fintechs and enable them to expand their reach to a wider audience. This development is particularly imperative in emerging economies, where numerous businesses and individuals are faced with barriers when wanting to access traditional financial services due to geographical and monetary constraints (Adel, 2023). Therefore, fintech solutions, such as mobile banking, peer-to-peer lending, and digital wallets, offer the potential for bridging that gap, which may provide low-cost, easily accessible financial services to underbanked and unbanked populations.

5.3 Fintech and Sustainable Finance

Fintechs and traditional financial institutions are increasingly integrating ESG principles, as well as Impact criteria, into their decision-making frameworks, with the objective of endorsing sustainability. Crowdfunding and distributed ledger technology represent domains wherein financial technology and sustainable finance may cooperate to further the cause of sustainability. Moreover, artificial intelligence and extensive data analysis are employed to scrutinize the ecological conduct of corporations. Financial technology constitutes a potential catalyst for the promotion of sustainable development and the alignment of financial practices with environmental objectives. For instance, within the agricultural sector, financial technology fosters sustainability by means of crowdfunding, digital transaction systems, and electronic marketplaces that facilitate connections among farmers, land proprietors, investors, and consumers. The interconnection between financial technology and sustainable finance bears considerable potential for the construction of sustainable communities, the encouragement of conscientious consumption and production, and the mitigation of impoverishment (Vergara & Agudo, 2021, pp. 7–10).

Results

4

In the following chapters, key findings that emerged from the qualitative interviews are presented. For a clear presentation, the following sub-sections correspond to the general layout of the interview guidelines. To proficiently showcase the outcomes of the interviews, a comparative analysis with emphasis on thematic focal points is employed, in alignment with the methodology proposed by Zurbriggen et al. (2018). In addition, the initial concept of the Impact Taxonomy is presented, which consists of both the top-down and bottom-up approach. To demonstrate the practical application of the bottom-up methodology, two illustrative cases are provided. Finally, the findings of the quantitative survey are summarized and analyzed in detail.

1 Evaluation of the Qualitative Interviews

Within the following chapters, the insights gained from the qualitative interviews are outlined and meticulously analyzed in accordance with the categories delineated in the interview guide.

1.1 Positive SDG Implications

The responses of the interviewees regarding positive SDG implications have a broad range from affecting a multitude of different SDGs to not being able to fully determine the relevant SDGs, which are positively affected by the business model. Some interviewees, for instance, highlighted potential benefits of fintechs in decreasing poverty, thereby having a positive effect on SDG 1, "No poverty", through the inclusion of people in financial activities and providing access to digital money, stablecoins, and mobile wallets, therefore positively affecting SDG 10 "Reduced Inequalities". Furthermore, it was also mentioned that fintechs and cryptocurrencies can contribute to digitalization, which leads to increased education around new

K. Wendt, M. Hauser, *Green FinTech*, Sustainable Finance,
https://doi.org/10.1007/978-3-031-78279-4_4

technologies and improves the quality of education, therefore positively affecting SDG 4 "Quality Education". Additionally, fintechs have a positive impact on SDG 8 "Decent work and economic growth" through the creation of new jobs and working models, particularly in developing countries, and specifically by providing access to financial services. Moreover, fintechs have a positive effect on SDG 9 "Industry, Innovation and Infrastructure" through fintech applications and blockchain technology. In addition to that, it was mentioned that fintechs have a positive effect on SDG 10 "Reduced Inequalities" through improved financial inclusion and access to financial services as well as a positive effect on SDG 11 "Sustainable cities and communities", for instance, by providing blockchain-based solar energy management systems. Furthermore, fintechs positively affect SDG 13 "Climate Action" through a reduction of emissions due to online operations compared to more energy-intensive traditional banking services, although the server usage might still have a negative impact. Lastly, fintechs can have a positive effect on SDG 17 "Partnership for the Goals" by contributing to the achievement of all 17 SDGs through industry-wide collaboration. Additionally, the interviewees mentioned secondary impacts on SDGs such as SDG 5 "Gender Equality" and the creation of sustainable cities and communities through smart city applications. In summary, it can be asserted that fintechs possess a wide array of favorable implications for SDGs.

1.2 Negative or Uncertain SDG Impact

With regard to negative effects on SDGs or uncertain implications, where no direct link can be identified, interviewees listed several SDGs with no direct impact implications and also some potentially negatively affected SDGs by the business model of the fintech. In relation to SDG 2 "Zero Hunger", it was stated that no direct impact can be identified, whereas the impact on SDG 3 "Good Health and Well-being" is uncertain as well and even potentially has an indirect negative effect due to one interviewee's fintech's products on their alternative investment platform containing alcoholic beverages. Whereas no direct impact on SDG 6 "Clean Water and Sanitation", SDG 7 "Affordable and Clean Energy", and SDG 12 "Responsible Consumption and Production" can be identified. Although one interviewee mentioned the intensive water consumption in alcohol production, therefore constituting a negative indirect effect on SDG 6 "Clean Water and Sanitation". Furthermore, the high energy consumption of Bitcoin mining constitutes a negative impact on SDG 13 "Climate Action". Although no direct impact can be identified on SDG 14 "Life Below Water" & SDG 15 "Life on Land" and SDG 16 "Peace, Justice and Strong Institutions". Furthermore, a negative impact was mentioned due to the increased electricity consumption of data centers and use of cars by employees in order to commute to the office, constituting a negative effect on SDG 7 "Affordable and Clean Energy" and SDG 13 "Climate Action". Overall, it can be determined that fintechs have negative direct and indirect impacts on multiple SDGs, which represent a conflict of objectives between each goal.

1.3 Identification of Key Performance Indicators

For defining Key Performance Indicators (KPIs), they must be relevant, available, replicable over time, reliable, valid, and thematically fitting to the topic. For instance, SDG 13 "Climate Action" could involve renewable energy production in kilowatt-hours and avoid CO_2 in tons. Fund diversity has an influence on the level of standardization in measuring impact; a more diverse fund will require different KPIs for each investment, which makes its standardization more challenging. Transparency and adaptability are critical aspects in measuring impact. However, the presence of diverse approaches should not be viewed as a negative aspect, due to the fact that these variances can foster greater innovation and efficacy in overall outcomes. In summary, it can be stated that KPIs must exhibit relevance, accessibility, long-term reproducibility, reliability, validity, and thematic alignment.

1.4 Impact Considerations in Fintech Formation

Impact generation as a core decision factor, when founding the business, has been discussed widely during the qualitative interviews, although some skeptical assessments were also mentioned. For instance, it was stated that during the initial phase fintechs are primarily focused on their daily business and survival, which takes precedence over considering the impact of their business. In contrast, it was also acknowledged that many fintechs have noble goals when founding the start-up but often get caught up in the economic reality and focus on making money and breaking even. Therefore, the focus during the challenging early phases of the startup lies on survival and managing resources effectively and pushes the impact generation into a secondary priority. Although, at a later stage, when the fintech arrives at a stable and successful position, the focus shifts more towards its original impact generation goals. This occurs mainly due to the fact that larger and well-established companies have more resources to consider impact goals. Furthermore, one interviewee believes that many people working on fintech projects consider impact goals implicitly, though not explicitly stated. Others described that their primary factor for founding the business was the tokenization and democratization of alternative investments, which therefore implies a conscious impact generation as a core founding factor. Moreover, one interviewee mentioned that the founding team was initially providing their financial products to themselves and their immediate circle, which led to the creation of the fintech itself. In conclusion, while some interviewees expressed the view that generating impact is a crucial consideration when establishing a business, others acknowledge that survival often takes precedence during the initial stages of fintech start-ups. It is worth noting that some fintechs may initially concentrate on financial objectives before transitioning towards impact generation once resources become available. Moreover, it is believed that numerous fintech projects implicitly take impact goals into account and certain firms strive to achieve impact right from the outset.

1.5 Adopting Impact Investing Frameworks

With regard to the overall adaptation of fintechs to Impact Investing Frameworks, the interviews revealed a considerable divergence among Swiss fintechs. Some interviewees are aware of the existence of Impact Investing frameworks but are not familiar with them in detail and believe that in the future, companies will have to fulfill certain criteria based on these frameworks. This is further solidified by the statement of other interviewees, who are familiar with the IRIS+ framework but not any other Impact Investing Framework. However, most interviewees are confident that sometime in the future, they will take measures and report on the impact of their fintechs. Whereas some interviewees have not yet come across Impact Investing Frameworks, as they are not familiar with such frameworks. Apart from this, divergent approaches to ESG and Impact Investing are not necessarily unfavorable, as they may be tailored to specific models. Moreover, the relevance of SDGs to fintechs was mentioned and the importance of addressing specific problems to contribute to SDGs. Consequently, it is advisable for an Impact taxonomy not to attempt to encompass the impact on all 17 SDGs, as these goals may, to some extent, conflict with one another. In addition, to develop a comprehensive impact taxonomy, it is imperative that the data collected is unambiguous and quantifiable, allowing for the evaluation of impact. Furthermore, certain data may be inherently subjective, thus rendering it challenging to interpret. In summary, Swiss fintechs have different familiarity states about Impact Investing Frameworks. Some respondent interviewees know about the frameworks but lack detailed knowledge about what they consist of. Other respondents are oblivious that the frameworks even exist. Various approaches to ESG and Impact Investing are seen as beneficial, allowing customization to specific models. The relevance of SDGs to fintechs was emphasized, suggesting that an Impact Taxonomy should focus on specific, quantifiable goals rather than attempting to address all 17 SDGs.

1.6 Investor Funding Criteria

Securing funding for a project is a vital step towards success. However, investors often have numerous specific criteria that they base their decisions on when choosing projects to invest in. The responses gained from interviewees were varied and several perspectives on what investors prioritize could be identified. For instance, it was stated that project governance and business success are some of the priorities of investors when choosing to fund a project. Although investors might not directly ask about specific impact criteria, they're generally concerned with whether the project is socially acceptable and if the potential for a return on investment exists. Furthermore, it was highlighted that funding criteria vary across different investors; some are genuinely focused on ESG factors, while others lean more towards Impact Investing. However, it was also noted that the distinction between the three GHG Protocol Corporate Standard emissions scopes is not always clear, and issues such as CO_2 emissions are increasingly of interest to many investors. Nonetheless, the distinction between direct and indirect emissions exists, but the discrepancy between Scopes 2 and 3 is still difficult to assess. Additionally, one interviewee stated they have not received funding from impact investors yet, but as they participate in a fintech incubator program that emphasizes on impact, they had several dedicated sessions on the topic. In conclusion, funding is essential for project success, with governance, business success, social acceptability, and return on investment at the center of investors' priorities. Moreover, the focus of investors varies tremendously; while some are mainly focused on ESG factors, others primarily focus on the generated impact. Lastly, issues with regard to emissions of a business are increasingly more important to investors, although the differentiation of emission scopes is often unclear.

1.7 Integration of ESG Elements in Firm Policies

With regard to the incorporation of ESG elements into firm policies, the interviewees revealed some surprising insights. For instance, one interviewee mentioned that they have adopted policies that not only concentrate on the business units but also include Human Resources aspects, such as hiring practices, for example. Consequently, their policies lack integrated ESG factors or impact-related elements. Besides that, others state that their scope rests primarily on governance with the intention to address ESG aspects in the future. However, they do have a detailed code of conduct and a control system in place. Consequently, these fintechs have incorporated certain intangible factors into their organizational policies, although without any explicitly defined ESG components. On the other hand, one interviewee indicated that in the case of start-ups, there is no need for tangible policies on sustainability since their concerns lie elsewhere and that they might even be having sustainable practices without stating them explicitly. It was also mentioned that governance and social issues matter more to fintechs since they are service-based and subject to high regulation. The environmental considerations might include electricity sourcing and appropriate business travel. Moreover, it was highlighted that the policy of a fintech should reflect the problems it addresses and deeply integrate them into the business processes. Furthermore, some interviewees support the use of existing frameworks and the alignment of policies with entities such as the 2X Challenge, the Science Based Targets Initiative, or the Carbon Disclosure Project. In summary, some fintechs have policies encompassing Human Resources and governance aspects without explicit ESG elements. Some interviewees suggest start-ups implicitly practice sustainable behaviors and thus may not need explicit sustainability policies. Others emphasize governance and social issues for service-based, regulated fintechs. One respondent suggests that fintechs' policies reflect the problems they tackle and align them with existing methodologies such as the 2X Challenge or the Carbon Disclosure Project.

1.8 Investment and Fundraising Policies

The importance of having a well-defined directive for investment and fundraising policies has been emphasized during the interviews. One interviewee, for instance, highlights the importance of having a well-defined internal directive for investment and fundraising policies, which they have implemented. Furthermore, others mentioned the need for due diligence in partner selection to ensure suitable investments, fair purchase prices, and proper storage and insurance. Moreover, it was claimed by one interviewee that they aim to reduce inequality and avoid investments that may not yield satisfactory returns. Whereas other interviewees discuss the advantages and disadvantages of using exclusion lists in investment policies. An impact expert further argued that defining specific goals and priorities of a fintech is crucial in deciding whether to use exclusion lists and choosing appropriate asset classes. Additionally, the impact expert suggested maintaining a broad approach when it comes to fundraising, as it allows for a wider range of investors and enhances the appeal of the investment solution. Besides that, it was recommended keeping an open mind and considering the potential benefits of various types of investments. In general, it can be asserted that the formulation of a thoroughly conceived investment and fundraising policy that incorporates pertinent ESG and Impact factors as is deemed reasonable by fintechs. Nonetheless, presently the majority of fintechs have not yet executed such measures in their entirety.

1.9 Addressing Investor Criticisms

Investing in fintechs is a complex decision-making process that requires investors to encompass several factors, which influence their investment choices. In order to understand this process, an exploration of the predominant criticisms expressed by investors has been undertaken, specifically with regard to the integration of ESG factors and impact-related considerations into their investment decisions. Based on the experience of some interviewees, investors generally tend to prioritize a fintech's potential for economic success above other factors. It was further expressed that the need to specifically inform and assure investors about a fintech's probability of success and showcase the ability to potentially achieve exponential growth is what most investors are looking for. Furthermore, investors are more inclined to support ventures that positively impact the environment and society without sacrificing profitability. Similarly, it was highlighted that investors are keen on understanding customer acquisition costs and the scalability of the user journey. Moreover, the need to clarify the due diligence process and ensure that products are offered at competitive market prices has been mentioned. According to one interviewee, the challenge lies in proving to investors that a specific investment amount will result in a particular number of customers. In a nutshell, investors criticize a project mostly regarding its profitability and scalability. They primarily focus on the possibility of success in ventures rather than solely focusing on ESG and impact factors. This shows that there is a need for fintechs to communicate in detail how precisely they balance success in the financial dimension and positive societal and environmental contributions to be able to sustain investor concerns.

1.10 Assessing Financial Inclusion Impact

Financial inclusion is a crucial aspect of ensuring economic growth and reducing poverty worldwide. As financial services and products become more accessible and comprehensible, more people can participate in the economy and benefit from it. With regard to measuring the impact of financial inclusion, the interviewees highlighted several specific indicators. For instance, it was stated that financial inclusion can be measured by the number of users accessing financial services and products and provided an example of how mobile banking apps enable people in remote areas to access banking services. Whereas some interviewees believe that having access to more information does not necessarily lead to a better understanding. Nonetheless, the significance of elucidating financial information in an uncomplicated and comprehensible manner to facilitate understanding among the general population was underscored. Furthermore, one interviewee advocated for the avoidance of technical terminologies and instead encouraged the breakdown of complex information into easily digestible chunks that can be grasped by a broad audience. As a provider of alternative investment solutions to retail customers, one interviewee mentioned measuring monthly active users and the average investment amount per customer as key indicators of their impact on financial inclusion. Whereas other interviewees suggest that financial inclusion can be also measured by the number of people who read educational articles, the number of people converted from an article into an investor base, and the granularity of new users' data. Besides that, the interviewee emphasized the importance of efficiency, cost reduction, speed, and information flow in addressing financial inclusion. In general, financial inclusion can be assessed using various indicators. However, it is important to note that the suggested criteria provide a superficial measurement of the impact and employing more granular and comprehensive approaches would yield greater insights into the actual impact generation.

1.11 Impact Disclosure in Mission Statements

Impact-related disclosures inside the mission statement are certainly a common way companies can inform their stakeholders about their commitment to create a positive impact. Unfortunately, one interviewee admitted a lack of awareness regarding disclosures related to impact generation within their company's mission statement. Nonetheless, another interviewee confirmed that their mission statement includes the democratization of the financial market, which they measure by observing the number of Monthly Active Users. Thus, in other words, most of the fintechs do not include impact-related disclosure in their mission statements. Moreover, those firms that have implemented such disclosures do not appear to measure them in a thorough and substantive manner.

1.12 Product Outcomes by Demographic Groups

Market segmentation is a vital aspect of developing products that cater to diverse groups of people with different needs and preferences. In this regard, one interviewee believes that analyzing product outcomes by key demographic groups can help a company improve and develop its products to reach more people. Furthermore, the importance of age, income gaps, and gender in product outcomes was mentioned. According to another interviewee, younger people tend to be more attracted to fintech products, and targeting lower-income individuals can help demonstrate the value of investing small amounts early on. The interviewee also highlights that women may be less interested in financial topics than men but can be engaged if the information is presented appropriately. Although, according to the interviewee, ethnicity is not considered a useful factor to target, while cultural factors might play a role. Nevertheless, one interviewee stated that their fintech does not analyze product outcomes by key demographic groups. Moreover, the interviewee believes that there are some restrictions with regard to gathering demographic data on customers but could not list them specifically. The fundamental strategy of their fintech is to provide users with the option to determine the data they choose to share. Therefore, users can initially open an account without undergoing the verification process, as per the regulatory guidelines, which necessitate verification only if the account is intended to be utilized for trading activities or meets certain threshold limits. Consequently, the fintech consciously abstains from requiring verification at the onset and instead mandates it at a later stage. It is pertinent to note that data collection is governed by relevant legislation and hence is not carried out arbitrarily. In summary, it can be observed that the assessment of product outcomes based on key demographic segments can enhance the information repository available to fintechs. This, in turn, aids in refining and customizing the product offering to cater to the specific needs of each group. However, it is noteworthy that not all fintechs in the sample presently incorporate the measurement of product outcomes based on key demographic groups as a mandatory process. Instead, they grant the users the autonomy to determine the data they wish to share based on the associated product offering and the relevant legal regulations.

1.13 Evaluating Product Affordability for Underserved Groups

Financial technology revolutionized the financial industry, as it introduced innovative ways to access financial services. One of the leading benefits of fintech applications is the reasonably cheap cost they offer in comparison to traditional services, therefore making it more affordable for a wide array of individuals. One interviewee mentioned that in general, compared to the traditional banking services, most fintech applications are developed with the primary aim to lower costs. Moreover, the interviewee acknowledges that affordability can be an important factor for gaining market share. In conclusion, it can be asserted that affordability stands as a crucial element in generating impact as a fintech.

1.14 Financial Literacy Tool Implementation

Financial literacy is a critical aspect of making informed investment decisions and managing personal finances. In the ever-changing and developing financial industry, financial education and transparency have become critical factors in building trust with potential users. One interviewee highlighted the importance of financial education as well as risk management and suggested that fintechs should openly share their financial knowledge and research in order to build trust. Additionally, according to another interviewee, financial literacy is crucial and transparency is essential in building trust. Moreover, one interviewee discussed their efforts to provide educational content through blogs and webinars and their plans to implement gamification and learning tools into their mobile application. In addition to the aforementioned points, several methods for gauging the enhancement of financial literacy were proposed. These methods include monitoring user engagement, performing multiple questionnaires over extended periods to determine the degree of improvement over time and leveraging educational materials to guide the learning process. In conclusion, it can be asserted that the implementation of financial literacy tools as a fintech can be a suitable strategy for increasing confidence in the target group while equipping them with the appropriate knowledge that is essential in making well-informed investment decisions.

1.15 Carbon Dioxide Emission Measurement

As the world becomes more aware of the environmental impact of various industries, including the fintech sector, the need for measures to reduce carbon emissions has become more pressing. One interviewee, for instance, mentioned that they do not measure CO_2 emissions from the fintech itself. Whereas other interviewees expressed that there isn't a satisfactory framework to measure CO_2 emissions in the fintech sector and that the discussion is often complicated and politically or ideologically charged. Furthermore, it was also highlighted that many innovators are sensitive to environmental concerns and try to do their best in terms of reducing emissions. Nonetheless, it was stated by one interviewee that they do not currently measure CO_2 emissions of the fintech itself and explained that their decision regarding leased office space was primarily made based on factors such as location price as opposed to prioritizing environmental considerations. Lastly, it was speculated that a fintech's largest sources of emissions are likely to be related to people's transportation and server operations. Furthermore, one interviewee put forth the suggestion that effectively managing Scope 1 and Scope 2 emissions within the financial services sector is a comparatively straightforward task. However, the complexity increases when accounting for Scope 3 emissions. With regard to measuring CO_2 emissions of the product offering, one interviewee confirmed that they currently do not measure the CO_2 emissions of their product offering. In summary, it can be observed that the primary factors contributing to direct CO_2 emissions of fintechs are associated with the operation of servers and the transportation of individuals, thereby falling under the purview of Scope 1 and Scope 2 emissions.

1.16 Analyzing Fintech Energy Efficiency and Consumption

As concerns about climate change and energy consumption continue to grow, there has been a greater emphasis on promoting energy efficiency in various industries, including the fintech sector. In this regard, one interviewee acknowledged that they do not determine the energy efficiency of their fintech, stating that startups need to prioritize other aspects such as liquidity. Moreover, the interviewee also mentioned the importance of having sufficient resources, both human and financial nature, to measure and report energy efficiency. Moreover, it was explained that technical aspects were more important when evaluating Google Cloud as a partner and admitted that functionality has been the most important criterion for their selection process. Additionally, one interviewee admitted that while they did not consciously focus on energy efficiency, they considered it when choosing server locations, but primarily concentrated on cost factors during the decision-making process. In conclusion, it can be asserted that the majority of fintechs within the sample understand the importance of energy efficiency, although they tend to place a greater emphasis on cost and liquidity management during the initial stages of a start-up.

1.17 Carbon-Intensive Industry Exposure Mitigation

Sustainability and responsible investment practices have become increasingly significant issues in the financial industry, with more investors looking to limit their exposure to carbon-heavy industries. In this regard, one interviewee mentioned that they do not currently focus on this aspect consciously, but they have considered the industries they invest in, such as the production of whisky. It is noteworthy that the aforementioned fintech operates within the alternative investment sector, specifically catering to retail investors who typically lack access to such investment opportunities. As per the interviewee's statements, they have recognized the necessity of providing private equity investments on their platform in the near future. Furthermore, they have expressed their commitment to avoid carbon-heavy industries. Besides that, the interviewee also stated their interest in investments that follow the theme of sustainability and are exploring carbon emission programs to offer such opportunities on their platform. Overall, it can be asserted that the mitigation of carbon-intensive industry exposure assumes a pivotal role. However, it is currently inadequately supported within the interview sample.

1.18 Implementing Risk Management Standards

With the continued rapid growth and changes in the fintech industry, the need for effective governance measures has drastically increased. One interviewee acknowledged that they currently do not measure the impact of governance-related measures. Besides that, the interviewee referred to having risk management and different KPIs in place, but none of them relate to ESG or impact generation. Similarly, the interviewee explained that their fintech has no ISO certification, due to the fact that most of the regulated aspects are handled through third-party companies such as data centers and compliance firms. While they do not have ESG components in their risk management, they do need to monitor around 150–160 KPIs in areas such as blockchain and compliance, with varying frequencies. Additionally, another interviewee also discussed using a classical risk management framework in which they continuously measure the impact, probability, and severity of individual dimensions. They do not have any certification or audits in place at present. However, as the company grows and is being sought after by larger investors, the pressure for certification and audit will increase, which ultimately pushes them towards the implementation of such measures. In summary, it is worth mentioning that the majority of fintech entities within the sample have established risk management standards, primarily concentrated on business-oriented KPIs and tailored to suit the size of the start-up at each developmental stage.

1.19 Fundamental Governance Principles

Good governance is a vital ingredient behind a thriving business, and fintech start-ups are increasingly under pressure to institute an optimal standard of good governance practices right from the founding. One interviewee emphasized that their company is regulated by FINMA, the Swiss Financial Market Supervisory Authority, and follows strict policies similar to those of banks, with stringent anti-money laundering regulations, among others. These policies are audited by external auditors. Additionally, another interviewee expressed that basic governance principles should be adopted when starting a business with regard to a clear division of roles and responsibilities, risk management, and control frameworks. In addition, the interviewee asserts that about 80% of such fundamental principles form the governance efforts, and the rest is added afterwards when the business grows. One interviewee added that governance of their infrastructures is sustained by a system of risk management as well as an internal control framework that is being measured periodically. Other than that, the importance of governance was also raised by another interviewee, citing an example of ensuring the board's independence, nurturing diversity, and establishing various committees to oversee specific areas of the operation within the organization. Furthermore, the importance of ESG being a topic at the board level was also discussed during the interviews and how this can affect executive salaries. In addition, one interviewee further emphasized the importance of governance in both listed and private companies and the need for compliance with laws. Likewise, one interviewee highlighted the value of diversity in an organization for better governance and the significance of having the right mix of people on board. Besides that, the requirement of incorporating the concept of sustainability within the organization structure in improving governance and perpetuating long-term success was emphasized during the interviews. In summary, it can be noted that it is imperative for Swiss fintechs to establish key governance principles, including clear division of roles, effective risk management, and compliance with regulations, early on in their operations. These principles should be subject to ongoing improvement and refinement. Furthermore, to ensure a highly functioning governance, it is crucial to establish board independence, diversity, and committees. The integration of ESG factors and diversity can significantly enhance governance and contribute to long-term success.

1.20 Compensation Policy Guidelines

In the highly competitive fintech industry, attracting and retaining talent is essential for success. In this regard, one interviewee explained that their compensation structure includes a monthly salary and an Employee Stock Option Plan (ESOP). They try to pay market salaries for younger employees, while higher-level employees might have a salary cap, which is supplemented by the stock option plan. Similarly, another interviewee mentioned that companies must be competitive in the market to attract and retain talent. Although salaries in the fintech industry are generally not exceptionally high compared to other sectors, they do meet the prevailing market standards. The focus is more on success-based compensation to reward employees for taking risks and contributing to the company's growth. Additionally, one interviewee emphasized that they pay for skills, with different grades and bands for various roles. The compensation structure is flexible and adjusts to the changing needs of the organization, as different skills become more or less relevant. Regarding the compensation policy, one interviewee stated that the compensation depends on the fintech's area of operation and can be focused on KPIs like revenue or sales, as well as environmental issues or diversity quotas. In conclusion, it can be noted that the compensation policies of the fintechs sampled are in adherence to industry standards for entry-level positions and encompass ESOPs for higher-level employees. Moreover, the compensation structure exhibits a flexible nature, wherein it adapts to the dynamic demands of the organization.

1.21 Audit Committee Structure Determination

In the fast-paced and dynamic fintech industry, governance and audit committees play an essential role in ensuring that companies adhere to strict regulations and ethical standards. Nonetheless, it is typically observed that smaller fintech firms lack an audit committee structure at present. For instance, one interviewee explained that their organization does not have an internal audit committee, as they are audited by third parties that follow a clear catalog from the FINMA. Although, there are checks conducted on an annual basis, as well as those that occur every 2 or 3 years. Apart from this, an Impact and ESG Specialist stated that when analyzing potential portfolio companies, they are focused on governance in relation to audit committees, discussing factors such as board independence, diversity, and the backgrounds of board members. Moreover, they are analyzing how ESG topics are discussed at the board level, including Sustainability Linked Compensation for executives. In summary, it can be observed that for fintech companies, the Audit Committee structure holds significant importance in evaluating portfolio firms in terms of their compliance with regulatory and ethical standards, as well as the integration of elements such as Sustainability-Linked Compensation for executives.

1.22 Navigating Novel Technological Regulations

Navigating novel technological regulations has become a significant challenge, such as artificial intelligence and the distributed ledger technology. One interviewee explained that the blockchain technology introduces an unprecedented way of establishing consensus without relying on a central authority or even people. This innovation has led to the emergence of decentralized autonomous organizations (DAOs) and other applications. Additionally, another interviewee discussed their efforts in leveraging blockchain technology while remaining compliant with regulations such as FINMA. Moreover, the interviewee mentioned Switzerland's sandbox environment for fintechs, which offers a supportive regulatory framework. Besides that, the interviewee highlighted the importance of existing regulations and anticipated their expansion in the forthcoming years. Furthermore, the interviewee addressed the potential hazards linked with custody and underscored the significance of maintaining assets off the company's balance sheet to safeguard investors, which corresponds to the fintech's approach. Lastly, the interviewee further suggested that forthcoming regulations may take into account such risks. In conclusion, it can be asserted that maintaining a comprehensive understanding of emerging technological regulations holds considerable advantages for fintechs aiming to streamline their compliance processes with forthcoming regulations.

1.23 Impact Analysis on Fintech Performance Metrics

The impact of sales, profit, and margins on fintechs can be challenging to determine, and it may depend on the focus of the company. For instance, one interviewee explained that it is challenging to determine the impact based on sales, profit, and margins of a fintech. Moreover, another interviewee emphasized that measuring the impact of sales, profit, and margins depends on whether the fintech has a focus on sustainable solutions. For fintechs with a sustainability focus, it makes sense to measure impact, while for others, it may not be relevant. With regard to the possibility to scale up the impactful part of the business, based on the sales, profit, and margins, one interviewee explained that scaling up may not result in increased transparency. Instead an Impact and ESG expert, highlighted that it would be preferable to have a clear separation between sustainable and non-sustainable aspects of a business. Moreover, the interviewee suggested that companies should focus on implementing action plans to improve the non-sustainable parts of their operations rather than just measuring the impact. In conclusion, it can be asserted that quantifying impact based on performance metrics like sales, profit, and margin is deemed problematic. Nevertheless, fintechs should prioritize establishing a conspicuous demarcation between sustainable and non-sustainable elements of their business, as well as formulating a well-defined action plan to rectify the non-sustainable aspects of their operations.

1.24 Active Ownership Board Composition Standards

Effective corporate governance is imperative for the success of any enterprise, and active engagement with the underlying portfolio firms, coupled with the ability to influence their decisions, holds a pivotal role in shaping the direction of the enterprise. In this regard, one interviewee described rules and guidelines to determine the impact of board composition for portfolio companies in terms of active ownership. For instance, according to the interviewee, companies should first define the business case, products, and services for the underlying portfolio companies and then identify the competencies needed at the board level for strategic guidance. Next, the company should seek people with those competencies. A crucial aspect is to maintain balance between engaged board members, such as the chairman and vice chairman and independent board members who can bring a fresh perspective to the table and positively influence the day-to-day business. In conclusion, it can be stated that for fintechs operating within the Open Finance industry, active engagement with the underlying portfolio companies and the ability to influence their decision-making processes hold crucial significance to achieve positive impact.

1.25 Country-Specific Business Condition Overview

The business conditions that prevail in a particular country can exert a significant impact on the level of innovation that is witnessed within this nation. In this regard, one interviewee mentioned that the general business conditions in a country play a significant role in fostering innovation, which in turn leads to societal change. Moreover, favorable conditions for innovation can have a leveraged impact on the status quo. While maintaining the same conditions may lead to limited progress. In other words, promoting innovation in the business environment is crucial for creating meaningful and lasting impact. In summary, it can be asserted that the prevailing business conditions within a country play a pivotal role in determining the extent to which innovation is fostered within its economic landscape.

1.26 Open Banking: Key Findings and Observations

Regarding the determination of relevant KPIs for Open Banking fintechs, one interviewee discussed the difficulty in determining KPIs by using credit card statements to evaluate sustainability, due to the difficulty in determining the use case of transactions, which would require totalitarian systems in order to incentivize desirable behaviors and discourage undesirable behaviors. The interviewee also notes that assessing the impact of digital services like TWINT on sustainability is not straightforward. One interviewee disclosed a collaborative project with the Lucerne University of Applied Sciences and Arts that centers around the development of a recommendation engine aimed at monitoring clients' environmentally conscious expenditure. Thus, this project is aimed at yielding invaluable insights towards improving their Sustainable expenditure habits that are aligned with their SDGs. It ought to be noted that now the project is at its development stage. Another interviewee suggested looking at the efficiency and security aspects of transactions as potential KPIs for fintechs, for instance, whether individuals reduce their travel or conduct transactions with greater speed and security. In relation to the product outcomes across various demographic segments, one interviewee affirms that the fintech systematically gathers and analyzes demographic data. Moreover, they proactively develop and provide tailored products and services catering to distinct demographic groups. Notably, among the offerings are specialized accounts aimed at enhancing financial literacy among children.

1.27 Open Finance: Key Findings and Observations

The interviewees explored various aspects of Impact Investing, including measuring investment impact on SDGs, determining relevant KPIs, applying different Impact Investing frameworks, assessing investors' funding criteria, implementing investment policies, evaluating CO_2 emissions, limiting exposure to carbon-intensive industries, and incorporating active ownership for diverse board compositions. One interviewee mentioned the difficulty in measuring impact on the investment level and the different approaches to doing so but reaffirmed using the IRIS+ taxonomy in order to determine the overall impact of the business because it can be used for different industries. Although this interviewee didn't see a significant difference in applying these frameworks in private equity or listed equities. Furthermore, the interviewee also mentioned that looking at the products of the fintech and determining the impact of these products on the SDGs would be a suitable approach. Regarding the measurement of CO_2 emissions of investments, some interviewees discussed Scope 1, 2, and 3 emissions, mentioning that Scope 3 are the most challenging to measure and interpret. In this regard, one interviewee emphasized the significance of comprehending and interpreting raw data, highlighting the need for acquiring the skills and expertise necessary to do so. This further underscores the importance of moving beyond a simple reliance on ratings and engaging in more nuanced and thorough analysis. Moreover, one interviewee stated elements KPIs should demonstrate, such as that they must be thematically fitting, available, replicable over time, valid, and reliable. The challenge with the Impact Fund of the interviewee's company is the variety of KPIs they track for different investments, as a Fund-of-Fund Private Equity Manager. According to the interviewee, it is important to be transparent and implement different approaches for Impact Investing. With respect to investors funding criteria, the interviewee expressed much interest in investees reporting on the issue of Scope 3 emissions but admitted that the figures associated with this criterion are difficult to interpret. This puts the question of whether such information can be effectively put into actual use by the investors or whether it is just a superficial process, a formality that pertains only to the need for a differentiation between the different scopes but does not provide an effective differentiation that provides a substantive analysis function to be fulfilled.

2 Impact Taxonomy

In the following chapter, the self-developed Impact Taxonomy, according to Fig. 4.1, will be presented and outlined. Firstly, the bottom-up approach, including each Impact Theme, Strategic Goal, and Key Performance Indicator (KPI) will be described for both the Open Banking and the Open Finance sector. Secondly, two cases for the application in practice will be presented in order to demonstrate the intended effect of the Impact Taxonomy. Lastly, the top-down approach, including each Impact Factor, Strategic Objectives, and Performance Indicators for the fintech level will be addressed.

2.1 Bottom-Up Approach Open Banking

Financial inclusion is one of the vital Impact Themes in the Impact Taxonomy for Swiss fintech, as it paves the way for the unbanked and underbanked population toward eventual increased financial health. Two strategic goals at the very center of

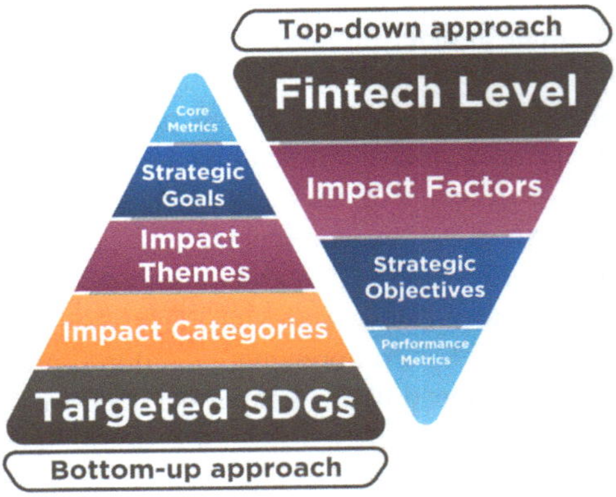

Fig. 4.1 Impact taxonomy approach. © Dr. Karen Wendt and Mathias Hauser, 2024

the theme are firstly enabling access to essential banking services and secondly better financial health. The KPIs maintain progress in these fields and outline which services are needed, tracking financial inclusion while improving the economic health of municipality residents by raising their credit score and debt-to-income ratio. Swiss fintechs, who concentrate on these strategic goals and KPIs, contribute to a more equal financial landscape and better overall economic well-being (Table 4.1).

Table 4.1 Bottom-up approach Open Banking (Financial Inclusion). © Dr. Karen Wendt and Mathias Hauser, 2024

Impact themes	Strategic goals	Core metrics (KPIs)
Financial inclusion	Enable access to basic banking services for unbanked and underbanked populations	<u>Outside-in perspective:</u> • Measuring the needs of unbanked and underbanked populations. (What services do you need to gain access to basic banking services?) <u>Inside-out perspective:</u> • Improvement in overall financial inclusion of municipality residents. • Reduction in reliance on informal financial services, leading to better financial regulation within the municipality. <u>Inside-in perspective:</u> • Increase in the number of unbanked and underbanked users accessing basic banking services through the platform. • Reduction in the percentage of unbanked and underbanked populations in the target region or country. • Percentage increase in financial products and services used by underserved populations. • Customer satisfaction rates among underserved populations.
	Improving financial health	<u>Outside-in perspective:</u> • Measuring the needs of users to enhance their financial well-being. (Which services are necessary to bolster your financial health status?) <u>Inside-out perspective:</u> • Improvement in overall financial health of municipality residents, measured by credit scores and debt-to-income ratios. <u>Inside-in perspective:</u> • Percentage of customers with reduced debt or increased savings. • Percentage of customers with increased financial resilience (e.g., emergency savings, insurance coverage).

Financial literacy has been incorporated to consistently gauge the impact by Swiss fintechs with regard to improving financial knowledge and skills in order to make sound financial decisions. Furthermore, financial literacy cements the need to empower the municipalities and their respective residents with the requisite knowledge and resources in making informed financial decisions. Two principal Strategic Goals are encompassed in this theme: developing tools and educational resources to enhance understanding and utilization of financial services and products and leveraging data to provide personalized insights and recommendations to facilitate better financial decision-making. By focusing on such strategic goals and employing corresponding KPIs, Swiss fintechs can cultivate better financial literacy and decision-making across municipalities. As such, they contribute to a more financially stable and prosperous society (Table 4.2).

Table 4.2 Bottom-up approach Open Banking (Financial Literacy). © Dr. Karen Wendt and Mathias Hauser, 2024

Impact themes	Strategic goals	Core metrics (KPIs)
Financial literacy	Develop tools and educational resources that help municipalities and their residents better understand and utilize financial services and products	Outside-in perspective: • Evaluate the current needs of users, which support them in understanding financial products. (What tools and educational resources do you need to improve your financial literacy?) Inside-out perspective: • Increase in financial literacy rates within municipalities through tools and educational resources usage. • Growth in local businesses and job opportunities, driven by improved financial knowledge and decision-making. Inside-in perspective: • User engagement with educational resources (e.g., time spent, completion rates, or quiz scores). • Increase in users' financial knowledge after using the platform (assessed through pre- and post-assessments).
	Leverage data to provide personalized insights and recommendations that promote better financial decision-making for municipalities	Outside-in perspective: • Determine the needs of users with regard to improving personalized recommendations in order to accomplish better financial decision-making. Inside-out perspective: • Adoption rate of personalized insights and recommendations for better financial decision-making. • Improved overall economic health of the municipality, driven by informed financial decision-making. Inside-in perspective: • Percentage of users who make improved financial decisions based on personalized insights. • User satisfaction with the quality and relevance of personalized recommendations.

Transparency is one key theme currently considered by which the generated impact by Swiss fintechs is consistently measured. It is noted that transparency is included as the foremost critical issue in offering clear and comprehensible transaction fees, service pricing structure, and interfaces in municipal financial services. This includes two critical strategic goals: improving transparency in transaction fees and pricing, as well as user-friendly interfaces for understanding and managing financial data. With a focus on these goals and using the respective KPIs, Swiss fintechs endeavor to bolster transparency, enabling better-informed financial decisions as part of a financial system that is more just and effective all at once (Table 4.3).

Table 4.3 Bottom-up approach Open Banking (Transparency). © Dr. Karen Wendt and Mathias Hauser, 2024

Impact themes	Strategic goals	Core metrics (KPIs)
Transparency	Improve transparency in transaction fees and pricing for municipal financial services	Outside-in perspective: • Measure the needs of users to improve the overall transparency and make the fees and pricing structure easily accessible and comprehensive. Inside-out perspective: • Reduction in transaction fees and increased pricing transparency for municipality residents. • Increase in municipal revenue through transparent transaction fees and lower pricing compared to traditional banking services. Inside-in perspective: • Improvement in user satisfaction regarding fee transparency, pricing, and product information. • Reduction in hidden fees or charges experienced by users.
	Create clear, user-friendly interfaces that enable municipalities to better understand and manage their financial data	Outside-in perspective: • Evaluate the needs of the users regarding user-friendly interfaces. (What kind of interfaces would support you most fundamentally in order to understand your financial data?) Inside-out perspective: • Increase in the number of users who successfully complete transactions, which is attributable to an ease of use and comprehension of the user interface. • Growth in the number of new users adopting the fintech solution, signifying that the user-friendly interface and transparency attract more customers. Inside-in perspective: • Percentage of users who report understanding their financial data and transaction history. • User satisfaction with the clarity and user-friendliness of platform interfaces.

Affordability has been incorporated as a core Impact Theme, emphasizing competitive and affordable financial services not only to the majority but also to the low-income and marginalized populations within the municipalities. Two major Strategic Goals underlie this theme: competitive pricing for value addition and affordable financial products catering to the underserved segments. In this regard, Swiss fintechs can strive to accomplish greater financial inclusion, a decrease in wealth and income inequality, and better financial health of their municipalities through such goals and the application of corresponding KPIs (Table 4.4).

Table 4.4 Bottom-up approach Open Banking (Affordability). © Dr. Karen Wendt and Mathias Hauser, 2024

Impact themes	Strategic goals	Core metrics (KPIs)
Affordability	Offer competitive pricing that enhances value for municipalities by reducing transaction fees for financial services	Outside-in perspective: • Determine the needs of users regarding competitive pricing. (What pricing of transaction fees would be appropriate for you?) Inside-out perspective: • Savings in transaction fees for residents, compared to traditional banking services. • Improved competitiveness of municipality financial services offerings. Inside-in perspective: • Average reduction in transaction fees or service costs for users. • Improvement in customer satisfaction ratings, reflecting enhanced value derived from competitive pricing.
	Promote affordable financial products that cater to low-income and marginalized populations within the municipality	Outside-in perspective: • Measure the needs of low-income and marginalized populations with regard to affordable financial products. (What would constitute affordable financial products for you?) Inside-out perspective: • Reduction in wealth and income inequality within the municipality. • Improvement in the overall financial health of low-income and marginalized communities, as affordable financial products facilitate better money management, saving, and credit-building opportunities. Inside-in perspective: • Number of low-income or marginalized users gaining access to affordable financial products and services. • Percentage increase in the usage of affordable financial products by the target population.

Efficiency has been identified as a relevant and important Impact Theme to assess the generated impact in this regard consistently. Efficiency, as a critical theme, brings about the aspect of streamlining the payment processes for the reduction of transaction times and improvement of cross-border money transfers for the municipalities. This theme harbors two significant strategic goals: streamlined payment processes to reduce transaction times and more efficient cross-border money transfers. Concentrating on such goals and using corresponding KPIs, Swiss fintechs strive to develop an adaptive, inexpensive, and time-saving financial environment that contributes to improving the financial activity of municipalities and thus the general economic development (Table 4.5).

Table 4.5 Bottom-up approach Open Banking (Efficiency). © Dr. Karen Wendt and Mathias Hauser, 2024

Impact themes	Strategic goals	Core metrics (KPIs)
Efficiency	Streamline payment processes and reduce transaction times for municipalities	Outside-in perspective: • Determine users' needs with regard to payment transaction times and processing efficiencies within the municipality. Inside-out perspective: • Reduction in payment transaction times and processing efficiencies within the municipality. Inside-in perspective: • Reduction in average transaction processing time. • User satisfaction with the speed and ease of payment processing.
	Facilitate faster and more efficient money transfers for municipalities, particularly across borders	Outside-in perspective: • Determine users' needs with regard to international payment transaction times and processing efficiencies within the municipality. Inside-out perspective: • Increase in cross-border money transfers and associated time and cost savings within the municipality. Inside-in perspective: • Reduction in cross-border money transfer times. • Cost savings for users due to more efficient money transfers.

The need for personalization, as a fundamental Impact Theme, was incorporated to ensure an ongoing test on the ability of the fintech industry to offer personalized solutions. This emphasizes personalization and the need to use further data in fashioning household- or enterprise-specific financial products and services. At the same time, it makes personalized financial advice and recommendations for the municipalities. In addressing these strategic goals and related KPIs, Swiss fintechs can increase financial literacy, drive economic resilience, better satisfaction with services, and increase engagement in the municipalities. Personalization, through innovative and flexible financial solutions, caters to the specific needs and preferences of different user segments and consequently advances more sustainable economic growth within municipalities (Table 4.6).

Table 4.6 Bottom-up approach Open Banking (Personalization). © Dr. Karen Wendt and Mathias Hauser, 2024

Impact themes	Strategic goals	Core metrics (KPIs)
Personalization	Utilize data to create personalized financial products and services for municipalities	Outside-in perspective: • Evaluate the needs of users for personalized financial products and services. (How should financial products and services be customizable in order to ensure adequate personalization?) Inside-out perspective: • Higher financial literacy within the municipality as a result of tailored financial products and services. • Higher overall economic resilience within the municipality by meeting the diverse financial needs of the municipality's residents which leads to a more resilient local economy. Inside-in perspective: • Higher customer retention and acquisition rates as a result of tailored financial products and services. • User satisfaction with personalized financial products and services. • Increase in user engagement with personalized offerings.
	Deliver customized financial advice and recommendations based on individual municipal preferences and goals	Outside-in perspective: • Measure users' needs with regard to customized financial advice and recommendations. (What advice do you need to achieve your goals?) Inside-out perspective: • Enhanced reputation of the municipality for providing innovative, personalized financial solutions to its residents. Inside-in perspective: • User satisfaction with customized financial advice and recommendations. • Percentage of users who achieve their financial goals based on personalized guidance.

Security has been identified as an essential Impact Theme that ensures a consistent approach to measuring the generated impact in protecting financial assets and information at the municipal level. Fintechs may focus on enhancing security measures, such as fraud detection and identity verification, toward building more resilient financial infrastructure for municipalities against security threats. Addressing the respective strategic goals and their corresponding KPIs, Swiss fintechs can work towards the realization of a reduction in fraudulent transactions and security incidents by their clients while increasing user confidence and trust in the security measures provided on the platform. Overall, this focus results in a more solid and reliable financial ecosystem (Table 4.7).

Table 4.7 Bottom-up approach Open Banking (Security). © Dr. Karen Wendt and Mathias Hauser, 2024

Impact themes	Strategic goals	Core metrics (KPIs)
Security	Enhance security measures, including fraud detection and identity verification, to protect municipal financial assets and information	Outside-in perspective: • Determine users' needs to ensure a high level of safety. (What measures should be implemented to assure a high level of security of user's funds?) Inside-out perspective: • Strengthened resilience of the municipality's financial infrastructure against security threats. Inside-in perspective: • Reduction in the number of fraudulent transactions or security incidents. • Increase in user confidence and trust in the platform's security measures.

Economic growth has been included as a crucial Impact Theme to measure perpetually and sustainably the local socio-economic impact of Swiss fintechs. By helping small businesses within municipalities to grow, fintechs allow them to access indispensable financial services and capital. Addressing the associated Strategic Goals and KPIs, Swiss fintechs aim to identify users' needs, subsequently increasing the number of small businesses accessing financial services and capital within the municipality, which leads to a growth of small businesses and ultimately leads to a more prosperous local economy (Table 4.8).

Table 4.8 Bottom-up approach Open Banking (Economic Growth). © Dr. Karen Wendt and Mathias Hauser, 2024

Impact themes	Strategic goals	Core metrics (KPIs)
Economic growth	Support the growth of small businesses within municipalities by enabling access to financial services and capital	<u>Outside-in perspective:</u> • Identify users' needs for supporting the growth of small businesses. (What services do you need to provide small businesses with access to financial services and capital?) <u>Inside-out perspective:</u> • Increase in the number of small businesses accessing financial services and capital within the municipality. <u>Inside-in perspective:</u> • Increase in the number of small businesses obtaining financial services and capital. • Percentage growth in the total amount of capital disbursed to small businesses on the platform.

Sustainability has been identified as a crucial Impact Theme that underpins the fact that in developing digital banking services, it's vital to keep municipalities sustainable with low environmental impacts. It reflects the increased focus worldwide on sustainability and environmental stewardship. Swiss fintechs are supported by these strategic goals and KPIs in establishing the needs of users for environmentally friendly digital banking services based on energy-efficient technologies to decrease risk from extreme weather events such as floods, storms, and heatwaves. These measures should lower the municipality's carbon footprint, paper consumption, and energy use and contribute to a more sustainable financial landscape and promote responsible environmental practices within the fintech sector (Table 4.9).

Table 4.9 Bottom-up approach Open Banking (Sustainability). © Dr. Karen Wendt and Mathias Hauser, 2024

Impact themes	Strategic goals	Core metrics (KPIs)
Sustainability	Develop digital banking services for municipalities that minimize environmental impact	<u>Outside-in perspective:</u> • Determine users' needs for developing digital banking services that minimize environmental impact. (What tools to minimize the environmental impact would be most beneficial to the municipality?) <u>Inside-out perspective:</u> • Reduction in the municipality's risk of extreme weather threats. • Reduction in the municipality's carbon footprint due to the adoption of digital banking services. <u>Inside-in perspective:</u> • Reduction in paper usage and energy consumption due to digital banking services. • Decrease in energy usage per customer or transaction, resulting from the adoption of energy-efficient technologies and practices within the platform's digital infrastructure.

Innovation is a vital Impact Theme since it points out the need to underpin the development of new technologies and solutions in the financial sector for the benefit of the municipalities. This particular theme reflects the commitment of the fintech industry to drive change and foster state-of-the-art technologies. By adhering to the corresponding Strategic Goals and KPIs, Swiss fintechs strive to identify customer needs in innovation, foster the implementation of new financial technologies, and eventually create a stable reputation for a municipality as an innovation center. Committing to innovation, therefore, cements the fintech landscape and ensures that the municipalities remain competitive and adaptive to a rapidly evolving financial ecosystem (Table 4.10).

Table 4.10 Bottom-up approach Open Banking (Innovation). © Dr. Karen Wendt and Mathias Hauser, 2024

Impact themes	Strategic goals	Core metrics (KPIs)
Innovation	Encourage the development of new technologies and solutions in the financial sector that benefit municipalities	Outside-in perspective: • Identify users' needs with regard to the development of new technologies and solutions in the financial sector. (What technologies would be necessary to improve innovation within municipality?) Inside-out perspective: • Number of new financial technologies and solutions introduced in the municipality. • Growth in the municipality's reputation as an innovation hub in the financial sector. Inside-in perspective: • Number of new technologies or solutions developed within the financial sector. • Volume of transactions processed using new payment solutions.

Gender equality is one of the critical Impact Themes to underline the importance of designing financial products and services around the unique needs of women and other underrepresented groups in municipalities. The theme depicts how Gender equality is one way the fintech industry commits itself to promoting inclusive access among the populace to financial services. In answer to those relevant Strategic Goals and KPIs, Swiss fintechs can aim to discern the needs of these groups, enhancing the municipality's reputation at the forefront of the gender equality and financial inclusion. These joint efforts contribute not only to social empowerment but also to economic opportunities, ensuring no segment of the population is left behind (Table 4.11).

Table 4.11 Bottom-up approach Open Banking (Gender Equality). © Dr. Karen Wendt and Mathias Hauser, 2024

Impact themes	Strategic goals	Core metrics (KPIs)
Gender equality	Design financial products and services that address the unique needs of women and other underrepresented groups within the municipality	Outside-in perspective: • Determine the needs of women and other underrepresented groups to increase gender equality. (What financial products and services would be most effective in reducing gender inequality?) Inside-out perspective: • Enhanced reputation of the municipality as a leader in promoting gender equality and financial inclusion. • Ways in which underrepresented groups benefited from the increase in gender equality, such as enhanced economic opportunities, social empowerment, improved access to financial services, and support for entrepreneurship. Inside-in perspective: • Increase in the number of female users or users from underrepresented groups accessing financial products and services. • Reduction in the gender or diversity gap within the user base of the platform. • User satisfaction with the inclusiveness and responsiveness of platform offerings.

Financial resilience is a paramount Impact Themes emphasizing the need for municipalities to support access to affordable financial products that help residents create emergency savings and manage unforeseen expenses. The theme signals the commitment of the fintech industry in boosting economic stability and empowering people to take steps in the face of financial uncertainties. By addressing the associated Strategic Goals and KPIs, Swiss fintechs aim to understand the user's needs and provide suitable solutions that increase the financial resilience of individuals. In this way, they contribute to an economically stable municipality and a decrease in the occurrence of economic crises among users, hence benefiting the wider community (Table 4.12).

Table 4.12 Bottom-up approach Open Banking (Financial Resilience). © Dr. Karen Wendt and Mathias Hauser, 2024

Impact themes	Strategic goals	Core metrics (KPIs)
Financial resilience	Enable municipalities to provide access to affordable financial products that help residents build emergency savings and manage unexpected expenses	Outside-in perspective: • Measure the needs of users to support them in building up emergency savings and manage unexpected expenses. (How could the fintech solution mostly ensure a higher financial resilience?) Inside-out perspective: • Increase in the percentage of individuals within the municipality with emergency savings and the ability to manage unexpected expenses. • Enhanced economic stability within the municipality due to increased individual financial resilience. Inside-in perspective: • Number of users who successfully build emergency savings or handle unexpected expenses. • Reduction in the occurrence of financial crises among users.

2.2 Bottom-Up Approach Open Finance

The central goal of financial inclusion as a key Impact Theme is to achieve more comprehensive access to investment options available for municipalities and the local business community, balanced with the need for regional economic development through local activities and encouraging alternative funding sources. Being included in the taxonomy shows the emphasis on bridging the financial gap to bring empowerment to more people and businesses so they can conduct economic opportunities. KPIs evaluate the effectiveness of different efforts in realizing financial inclusion and financial health within municipalities. Thus, by addressing these Strategic Goals and KPIs, Swiss fintechs can look forward to realizing a more inclusive and vibrant financial ecosystem that bolsters economic stability and development for all community members (Tables 4.13 and 4.14).

Table 4.13 Bottom-up approach Open Finance (Financial Inclusion). © Dr. Karen Wendt and Mathias Hauser, 2024

Impact themes	Strategic goals	Core metrics (KPIs)
Financial inclusion	Expand access to investment opportunities for municipalities and local businesses	Outside-in perspective: • Determine the needs of individuals and small businesses to access investment opportunities. (What solutions are missing in order to increase financial inclusion within the municipality?) Inside-out perspective: • Increase in the number of individuals and small businesses accessing investment opportunities within the municipality. • Enhanced reputation of the municipality with regard to financial inclusion and equal opportunities. Inside-in perspective: • Increase in the number of unbanked and underbanked users accessing finance and investment services through the platform, who previously had no access to such services. • Increase in total assets under management (AuM) from previously underserved segments.
	Enable community members to participate in regional economic growth by facilitating investment opportunities in locally focused enterprises, such as through thematic investments and direct, on-the-ground initiatives	Outside-in perspective: • Measuring the need of community members to participate in regional economic growth and identifying possible hurdles. (What services do you need to fully participate in locally focussed investment opportunities?) • Increase in the number of locally focused enterprises receiving investments from community members. • Growth in regional economic development driven by investments in local businesses and initiatives. Inside-out perspective: • Enhanced regional economic stability and diversification as a result of increased investment in local enterprises. • Increased local spending and circulation of funds within the municipality, boosting economic growth and development. • Growth in the local start-up and business ecosystem (e.g., Agriculture, Medicare, etc.) Inside-in perspective: • Number of community members successfully onboarded and educated about local investment opportunities. • Adoption and usage rates of the fintech's platform for facilitating investments in locally focused enterprises. • Number of successful local projects and enterprises funded through the fintech's platform, showcasing the effectiveness of the fintech's approach to supporting regional economic growth.

Table 4.14 Bottom-up approach Open Finance (Financial Inclusion). © Dr. Karen Wendt and Mathias Hauser, 2024

Impact themes	Strategic goals	Core metrics (KPIs) continued
Financial inclusion	Develop platforms that support alternative financing options, such as microfinance and crowdfunding, for municipalities and their residents	Outside-in perspective: • Determine users' needs for alternative financing options. (What financing options are currently missing and what financing options would increase financial inclusion within the municipality?) Inside-out perspective: • Growth in the use of alternative financing options, such as microfinance and crowdfunding, within the municipality and the outcome based on the achievements and tangible benefits derived from these initiatives. Inside-in perspective: • Number of alternative financing options supported on the platform (e.g., microfinance, crowdfunding). • Total funds raised or invested through alternative financing options on the platform.
	Improving financial health for municipalities	Outside-in perspective: • Measuring the needs of users to enhance their financial well-being (Which services are necessary to bolster your financial health status?) Inside-out perspective: • Reduction in the number of financially vulnerable individuals within the municipality, as indicated by a decrease in those living in poverty or experiencing financial hardships. • Improvement in the overall economic well-being of the municipality's population as a result of better financial health, demonstrated through increased economic activity and reduced reliance on social support programs. Inside-in perspective: • Percentage of customers with reduced debt or increased savings. • Percentage of customers with increased financial resilience (e.g., emergency savings, insurance coverage).

Enabling user-friendly and accessible financial literacy materials for municipalities is a core objective of this Impact Theme since it will allow informed decision-making and optimize financial management. Besides that, personalized advice on long-term financial planning and wealth management is important to provide sustainable growth and stability. Further included in the taxonomy is empowering the individual and businesses with the required knowledge and ability to navigate the intricacies of finance. Swiss fintechs can aim to tackle these strategic goals and KPIs to contribute to an improvement of financial literacy that ultimately results in a financially healthy and educated community (Table 4.15).

Table 4.15 Bottom-up approach Open Finance (Financial Literacy). © Dr. Karen Wendt and Mathias Hauser, 2024

Impact themes	Strategic goals	Core metrics (KPIs)
Financial literacy	Provide user-friendly platforms with accessible financial education materials, enabling municipalities to make informed decisions and optimize financial management	Outside-in perspective: • Determine users' needs with regard to how the platform should provide accessible financial education materials. (What elements does the platform need to incorporate in order for you to improve your financial literacy?) Inside-out perspective: • Improvement in financial literacy levels among municipality residents. • Strengthened financial well-being of the municipality's population through enhanced financial literacy and planning. Inside-in perspective: • User engagement with financial education materials on the platform (e.g., views, shares, completion rates). • Improvement in user financial knowledge and skills, as assessed by surveys or quizzes (pre- and post-assessments).
	Offer tailored advice to support long-term financial planning and wealth management for municipalities, fostering sustainable growth and stability	Outside-in perspective: • Identify the user's needs for offering them tailored advice to support long-term financial planning and wealth management. (How does the advice need to be in order to provide you with appropriate advice?) Inside-out perspective: • Attraction of talent and investment to the municipality due to its focus on financial literacy and education. • Strengthened financial well-being of the municipality's population through enhanced financial literacy and planning. Inside-in perspective: • Number of clients receiving tailored advice for long-term financial planning and wealth management, who previously had no access to such advice. • Improvement in clients' financial performance indicators (e.g., portfolio growth, diversification).

The main aim of transparency as an Impact Theme, primarily related to Open Finance, is to increase transparency in investment fees, risks, and product information – all while informing municipalities to make informed investment decisions. Inclusion in the taxonomy highlights the significance of instilling a culture of open communication, where trust prevails. Swiss fintechs can address these Strategic Goals and KPIs in order to boost their reputation by being at the forefront of transparent communication within the Open Finance ecosystem. In the long run, this should lead to increased user satisfaction and lowered hidden fees, as the whole financial ecosystem will become more responsible and accessible (Table 4.16).

Table 4.16 Bottom-up approach Open Finance (Transparency). © Dr. Karen Wendt and Mathias Hauser, 2024

Impact themes	Strategic goals	Core metrics (KPIs)
Transparency	Improve transparency in investment fees, risks, and product information, allowing municipalities to make well-informed investment choices	Outside-in perspective: • Measure the needs of users to improve the overall transparency and make the investment fees, investment risks, and product information easily accessible and comprehensive. (How should the investment fees, investment risks, and product information be outlined in order to ensure a high level of transparency?) Inside-out perspective: • Enhanced reputation of the municipality as a leader in promoting transparency in the asset management sector. Inside-in perspective: • Improvement in user satisfaction regarding fee transparency, investment risks, and product information. • Reduction in hidden fees or charges experienced by users.

The primary objective of affordability as an important Impact Theme is to develop low-cost and high-value asset management solutions that enable municipalities to optimize their financial resources toward achieving their investment targets. Affordability speaks to democratizing access to financial services and building up financial resilience for municipalities. By incorporating the outlined Strategic Goals and KPIs Swiss fintechs strive to develop efficient, accessible, and affordable platforms to ease the investment process that will translate into customer satisfaction and increased diversified investment options for municipalities (Table 4.17).

Table 4.17 Bottom-up approach Open Finance (Affordability). © Dr. Karen Wendt and Mathias Hauser, 2024

Impact themes	Strategic goals	Core metrics (KPIs)
Affordability	Develop low-cost, high-value asset management solutions that empower municipalities to maximize their financial resources and meet their investment objectives	Outside-in perspective: • Determine the needs of users to maximize their financial resources and meet their investment objectives. (How can the asset management solution empower municipalities to maximize their financial resources?) Inside-out perspective: • Enhanced efficiency in the allocation of municipal resources results in the liberation of capital, which can subsequently be designated for alternative municipal applications. Inside-in perspective: • Comparison of platform fees and costs with industry and traditional finance benchmarks. • Increase in the number of low-cost investment options on the platform.
	Create affordable platforms that simplify the process of discovering and selecting suitable investment products for municipalities	Outside-in perspective: • Determine the needs of users to simplify the process of discovering and selecting suitable investment products. (How can the platform simplify the process of discovering and selecting suitable investment products?) Inside-out perspective: • Increased investment diversification and financial resilience for municipalities. • Reduction in the time required for municipalities to identify suitable investment products. • Improved satisfaction among municipalities with available investment options. Inside-in perspective: • Number of affordable investment products available on the platform. • Improvement in user satisfaction with affordability and access to financial products and services.

Efficiency is a prominent theme in the impact taxonomy, particularly with regard to Open Finance, since the key objective is to drive efficiency with high levels of automation of the investment and financial management process. Consequently, this will result in reduced costs and improve the general effectiveness for municipalities. Including efficiency in the taxonomy will bring out the critical dimension of resource allocation that ensures better risk management and portfolio construction, thereby building further financial resilience for the municipalities. Through the use of the outlined Strategic Goals and KPIs, Swiss fintechs aim to utilize cutting-edge technology to achieve superior user experience and enable robust and balanced investment portfolios for municipalities (Table 4.18).

Table 4.18 Bottom-up approach Open Finance (Efficiency). © Dr. Karen Wendt and Mathias Hauser, 2024

Impact themes	Strategic goals	Core metrics (KPIs)
Efficiency	Implement advanced automation in investment and financial management processes to reduce costs and improve efficiency for municipalities	Outside-in perspective: • Identify users' needs to improve efficiency for municipalities. (How can the efficiency for municipalities be improved?) Inside-out perspective: • Enhanced ability of municipalities to allocate resources to priority projects. • More effective financial management within municipalities. Inside-in perspective: • Improvement in user experience and satisfaction with the platform's efficiency and speed, compared to industry benchmarks. • Improvement of the onboarding duration for new users on the investment platform.
	Utilize cutting-edge technology to enhance risk management and portfolio construction, enabling municipalities to build resilient investment portfolios	Outside-in perspective: • Determine the need of users to enhance optimal portfolio construction (How can efficient portfolios enable municipalities to build resilient investment portfolios?) Inside-out perspective: • Improved risk-adjusted returns for municipal investment portfolios. • Enhanced financial resilience for municipalities. Inside-in perspective: • Increase in the number of users benefiting from optimized portfolio construction. • Improvement in risk-adjusted investment returns.

Personalization, as one of the Impact Themes, underpins the significance of tailoring investment strategies as well as services for financial planning to the specific individual requirements of the municipality. The objective idea is to realign the investment portfolios with the strategic objectives, whereby the municipalities can realize their goals through proper financial planning. Adapting to the various Strategic Goals and KPIs, Swiss fintechs can build adaptable platforms that keep evolving with the changing needs and situations of their clientele to offer an exquisite experience in the dynamic financial landscape (Table 4.19).

Table 4.19 Bottom-up approach Open Finance (Personalization) © Dr. Karen Wendt and Mathias Hauser, 2024

Impact themes	Strategic goals	Core metrics (KPIs)
Personalization	Provide customized investment strategies and financial planning services that cater to the specific needs and priorities of each municipality	Outside-in perspective: • Identify the users' need for customized investment strategies. (How can financial planning services provide personalized offers to support municipalities?) Inside-out perspective: • Improved alignment between municipal investment portfolios and strategic objectives. • Strengthened ability to achieve strategic goals through effective financial planning. Inside-in perspective: • Growth in the number of clients receiving personalized investment strategies and financial planning services, who formerly lacked access to these resources. • Improvement in client satisfaction with personalization and relevance of services.
	Develop platforms that adapt to the changing needs and circumstances of municipalities, ensuring continued relevance and value	Outside-in perspective: • Determine the users' need to adapt to the changing needs and circumstances. (How can platforms ensure continued relevance and value?) Inside-out perspective: • Improved ability of municipalities to respond to changing circumstances and needs. Inside-in perspective: • Adaptability of the platform to user needs and circumstances, as measured by feedback and engagement metrics. • Number of platform features that adapt to user preferences and behaviors.

Security is an important Impact Theme in the domain of Open Finance, due to the fact that robust cybersecurity infrastructures offer a high level of municipal data and financial asset protection against potential threats and vulnerabilities. This strong emphasis on security has the potential to elevate further a municipality's reputation as a vigilant custodian of financial assets. With the adopted stated strategic goals and KPIs, Swiss fintechs could be among those experiencing fewer security incidents or breaches. This focus realizes increased confidence and trust among users in the measures put in place for the security of their platform (Table 4.20).

Table 4.20 Bottom-up approach Open Finance (Financial Security). © Dr. Karen Wendt and Mathias Hauser, 2024

Impact themes	Strategic goals	Core metrics (KPIs)
Security	Prioritize robust cybersecurity infrastructure to ensure the protection of municipal data and financial assets from potential threats and vulnerabilities	Outside-in perspective: • Determine the users' need for a robust cybersecurity infrastructure. (How can the platform protect municipal data and financial assets?) Inside-out perspective: • Enhanced reputation of municipalities for safeguarding financial assets. Inside-in perspective: • Number of security incidents or breaches, with a focus on minimizing occurrences, compared to industry benchmarks. • Increase in user confidence and trust in the platform's security measures.

Economic growth is an essential Impact Theme within the Open Finance domain, as delivering access to capital for entrepreneurs and start-ups within municipal jurisdictions drives innovation and job creation. By implementing the corresponding Strategic Goals and KPIs, Swiss fintechs have the potential to foster growth for local businesses and ultimately increase the overall business ecosystem, which will further strengthen the reputation of municipalities as a supportive environment for entrepreneurship and innovation. The impacts of this fintech activity are tracked by measuring the increase in capital raised by entrepreneurs and start-ups on the platform and the growth in job creation through supported businesses (Table 4.21).

Table 4.21 Bottom-up approach Open Finance (Economic Growth). © Dr. Karen Wendt and Mathias Hauser, 2024

Impact themes	Strategic goals	Core metrics (KPIs)
Economic growth	Promote access to capital for entrepreneurs and startups within municipal jurisdictions, spurring innovation and job creation	Outside-in perspective: • Determine the users' need to promote access to capital. (How can the fintech promote access to capital and spur innovation and job creation within the municipality?) Inside-out perspective: • Growth in the number of successful local start-ups and business ecosystem as well as job creation. • Enhanced reputation of municipalities as supportive environments for innovation and entrepreneurship. Inside-in perspective: • Increase in the amount of capital raised by entrepreneurs and startups on the platform. • Growth in the number of jobs created through supported businesses.

Sustainability is a central Impact Theme, with the drive to harness capital towards sustainable and responsible investments that support municipalities to accomplish long-term financial and environmental objectives. It also increases the reputation of municipalities as responsible investors and fosters their commitment to sustainable practices. To ensure the generated impact is measured consistently, Swiss fintechs therefore have the opportunity to monitor the increase in AuM allocated to sustainable and responsible investments and can determine the advance in ESG and impact ratings of investments made through the platform (Table 4.22).

Table 4.22 Bottom-up approach Open Finance (Sustainability). © Dr. Karen Wendt and Mathias Hauser, 2024

Impact themes	Strategic goals	Core metrics (KPIs)
Sustainability	Drive capital towards sustainable and responsible investments, supporting municipalities	Outside-in perspective: • Determine the users' need to drive capital towards sustainable and responsible investments. (How can the fintech drive capital towards sustainable and responsible investments and support municipalities?) Inside-out perspective: • Improved long-term financial and environmental outcomes for municipalities. • Enhanced reputation of municipalities as responsible investors. Inside-in perspective: • Increase in AuM allocated to sustainable and responsible investments. • Improvement in environmental, social, and governance (ESG) and impact ratings of investments made through the platform.

Innovation is a crucial Impact Theme as it allows fintechs to advance by leveraging novel technologies such as blockchain and artificial intelligence. Developing these platforms would enable fintechs to deliver novel financial solutions tailor-made to address the specific needs of municipalities. Inclusion in the taxonomy ensures that those technological advancements will lead to increased scalability, growth, and digitalization within municipal operations. Moreover, innovation can further boost an increased level of data-driven decision-making. KPIs measuring the generated impact are the adoption of emerging technologies among the platform operations as well as the number of innovative financial products and services launched on the platform (Table 4.23).

Table 4.23 Bottom-up approach Open Finance (Innovation). © Dr. Karen Wendt and Mathias Hauser, 2024

Impact themes	Strategic goals	Core metrics (KPIs)
Innovation	Develop platforms that leverage emerging technologies, such as blockchain and AI, to create innovative financial solutions for municipalities	<u>Outside-in perspective:</u> • Determine the users' need to develop platforms that leverage emerging technologies. (How can fintechs create innovative financial solutions for municipalities?) <u>Inside-out perspective:</u> • Enhanced capacity for scalability and growth in municipal operations, enabled by technology-driven platforms. • Increased digitalization and process automation rates within municipalities through the adoption of emerging technologies. • Improvement in data-driven decision-making capabilities for municipalities using the technology platforms. • Higher rate of innovation in municipal services and programs as a result of leveraging emerging technologies. <u>Inside-in perspective:</u> • Adoption of emerging technologies (e.g., blockchain, AI) within the platform's operations and solutions. • Number of innovative financial products and services launched on the platform.

Gender equality is a pivotal Impact Theme as the development of investment products that support gender equality within municipal jurisdictions fosters a more inclusive investment landscape. The inclusion of this theme in the taxonomy seeks to improve social outcomes related to gender equality within municipalities by encouraging fintechs to direct capital towards ventures promoting gender diversity. KPIs employed to gauge the generated impact include growth in AuM allocated to investment products supporting gender equality and improvement in gender diversity metrics among businesses supported by the investment platform (Table 4.24).

Table 4.24 Bottom-up approach Open Finance (Gender Equality). © Dr. Karen Wendt and Mathias Hauser, 2024

Impact themes	Strategic goals	Core metrics (KPIs)
Gender equality	Develop investment products that support gender equality within municipal jurisdictions, fostering an inclusive investment landscape	Outside-in perspective: • Determine the users' need to develop investment products that support gender equality. (What can the fintech do to support gender equality within municipal jurisdictions?) Inside-out perspective: • Improved social outcomes related to gender equality within municipalities. Inside-in perspective: • Growth in AuM allocated to investment products supporting gender equality. • Improvement in gender diversity metrics among businesses supported by the investment platform.

Financial resilience is an essential Impact Theme since offering financial education and advisory services supports long-term financial planning and wealth management for municipalities, empowering them to build a prosperous future for their communities. The inclusion of this theme aims to enhance long-term financial planning and performance for municipalities, as well as strengthen their capacity to effectively manage financial resources and meet strategic objectives. KPIs to assess the impact include growth in the number of users receiving financial education and advisory services, improvement in user financial stability indicators, and user preparedness for and resilience to economic shocks and financial challenges (Table 4.25).

Table 4.25 Bottom-up approach Open Finance (Financial Resilience). © Dr. Karen Wendt and Mathias Hauser, 2024

Impact themes	Strategic goals	Core metrics (KPIs)
Financial resilience	Offer financial education and advisory services that support long-term financial planning and wealth management for municipalities, empowering them to build a prosperous future for their communities	Outside-in perspective: • Determine the users' need for offering financial education and advisory. (How can fintechs support municipalities with long-term financial planning and wealth management?) Inside-out perspective: • Enhanced long-term financial planning and performance for municipalities. • Strengthened capacity to effectively manage financial resources and meet strategic objectives.

(continued)

Table 4.25 (continued)

Impact themes	Strategic goals	Core metrics (KPIs)
		Inside-in perspective: • Growth in the number of users receiving financial education and advisory services for long-term financial planning and wealth management. • Improvement in user financial stability indicators (e.g., savings rate, debt-to-income ratio). • Improvement in user preparedness for and resilience to economic shocks and financial challenges, as assessed by surveys or feedback.

2.3 Case 1 Open Finance: Robo-Advisory Provider

Fintechs operating in the robo-advisory space can contribute to several SDGs. The following breakdown illustrates the SDGs, which are mostly affected by the business model of a robo-advisory provider and shows how impact is being generated (Table 4.26).

Table 4.26 Impact taxonomy application Case 1. © Dr. Karen Wendt and Mathias Hauser, 2024

SDG	Impact theme	Strategic goal	Core metrics
SDG 1	Affordability	Develop low-cost, high-value asset management solutions that empower municipalities to maximize their financial resources and meet their investment objectives	Outside-in perspective: • Determine the needs of users to maximize their financial resources and meet their investment objectives. (How can the asset management solution empower municipalities to maximize their financial resources?) Inside-out perspective: • Enhanced efficiency in the allocation of municipal resources results in the liberation of capital, which can subsequently be designated for alternative municipal applications. Inside-in perspective: • Comparison of platform fees and costs with industry and traditional finance benchmarks. • Increase in the number of low-cost investment options available on the platform.

(continued)

Table 4.26 (continued)

SDG	Impact theme	Strategic goal	Core metrics
SDG 8	Economic growth	Promote access to capital for entrepreneurs and startups within municipal jurisdictions, spurring innovation and job creation	Outside-in perspective: • Determine the users' need to promote access to capital. (How can the fintech promote access to capital and spur innovation and job creation within the municipality?) Inside-out perspective: • Growth in the number of successful local start-ups and business ecosystem as well as job creation. • Enhanced reputation of municipalities as supportive environments for innovation and entrepreneurship. Inside-in perspective: • Increase in the amount of capital raised by entrepreneurs and startups on the platform. • Growth in the number of jobs created through supported businesses.
SDG 9	Innovation	Develop platforms that leverage emerging technologies, such as blockchain and AI, to create innovative financial solutions for municipalities	Outside-in perspective: • Determine the users' need to develop platforms that leverage emerging technologies. (How can fintechs create innovative financial solutions for municipalities?) Inside-out perspective: • Enhanced capacity for scalability and growth in municipal operations, enabled by technology-driven platforms. • Increased digitalization and process automation rates within municipalities through the adoption of emerging technologies. • Improvement in data-driven decision-making capabilities for municipalities using the technology platforms. • Higher rate of innovation in municipal services and programs as a result of leveraging emerging technologies. Inside-in perspective: • Adoption of emerging technologies (e.g., blockchain, AI) within the platform's operations and solutions. • Number of innovative financial products and services launched on the platform.

(continued)

Table 4.26 (continued)

SDG	Impact theme	Strategic goal	Core metrics
SDG 10	Financial inclusion	Expand access to investment opportunities for municipalities and local businesses	<u>Outside-in perspective:</u> • Determine the needs of individuals and small businesses to access investment opportunities. (What solutions are missing in order to increase financial inclusion within the municipality?) <u>Inside-out perspective:</u> • Increase in the number of individuals and small businesses accessing investment opportunities within the municipality. • Enhanced reputation of the municipality with regard to financial inclusion and equal opportunities. <u>Inside-in perspective:</u> • Increase in the number of unbanked and underbanked users accessing finance and investment services through the platform, who previously had no access to such services. • Increase in total assets under management (AuM) from previously underserved segments.
SDG 12	Sustainability	Develop digital banking services for municipalities that minimize environmental impact	<u>Outside-in perspective:</u> • Determine users' needs for developing digital banking services that minimize environmental impact. (What tools to minimize the environmental impact would be most beneficial to the municipality?) <u>Inside-out perspective:</u> • Reduction in the municipality's risk of extreme weather threats. • Reduction in the municipality's carbon footprint due to the adoption of digital banking services. <u>Inside-in perspective:</u> • Reduction in paper usage and energy consumption due to digital banking services. • Decrease in energy usage per customer or transaction, resulting from the adoption of energy-efficient technologies and practices within the platform's digital infrastructure.

Targeted SDGs

Fig. 4.2 SDG 1

SDG 1—No Poverty: By offering affordable and accessible investment services, robo-advisors can help low-income individuals build wealth over time, contributing to poverty alleviation efforts within the municipality (Fig. 4.2).

Fig. 4.3 SDG 8

SDG 8—Decent Work and Economic Growth: Robo-advisors can facilitate access to investments in small and medium-sized enterprises (SMEs), promoting economic growth and job creation (Fig. 4.3).

Fig. 4.4 SDG 9

SDG 9—Industry, Innovation, and Infrastructure: By making it easier for individuals and institutions to invest in infrastructure projects, robo-advisors can help mobilize resources to support sustainable industrialization and technological innovation (Fig. 4.4).

Fig. 4.5 SDG 10

SDG 10—Reduced Inequalities: Robo-advisory services can contribute to reducing inequalities by democratizing access to financial services and investment opportunities for underprivileged or marginalized populations (Fig. 4.5).

Fig. 4.6 SDG 12. Source SDGs: (United Nations, 2020)

SDG 12—Responsible Consumption and Production: Many robo-advisors now offer environmentally responsible and socially conscious investment options, encouraging sustainable consumption and production patterns among investors (Fig. 4.6).

2.4 Case 2 Open Banking: Provider of Payments and Cross-Border Transactions

Providers of instant payment solutions and cross-border transaction services affect a multitude of SDGs by their business model. The following overview illustrates which SDGs are mostly affected by the business model of an instant payment and cross-border transaction provider and how impact is being generated (Table 4.27).

Table 4.27 Impact taxonomy application Case 2. © Dr. Karen Wendt and Mathias Hauser, 2024

SDG	Impact theme	Strategic goal	Core metrics
SDG 1	Affordability	Offer competitive pricing that enhances value for municipalities by reducing transaction fees for financial services	Outside-in perspective: • Determine the needs of users regarding competitive pricing. (What pricing of transaction fees would be appropriate for you?) Inside-out perspective: • Savings in transaction fees for residents, compared to traditional banking services. • Improved competitiveness of municipality financial services offerings. Inside-in perspective: • Average reduction in transaction fees or service costs for users. Improvement in customer satisfaction ratings, reflecting enhanced value derived from competitive pricing
SDG 8	Economic growth	Support the growth of small businesses within municipalities by enabling access to financial services and capital	Outside-in perspective: • Identify users' needs for supporting the growth of small businesses. (What services do you need to provide small businesses with access to financial services and capital?) Inside-out perspective: • Increase in the number of small businesses accessing financial services and capital within the municipality. Inside-in perspective: • Increase in the number of small businesses obtaining financial services and capital. Percentage growth in the total amount of capital disbursed to small businesses on the platform

(continued)

Table 4.27 (continued)

SDG	Impact theme	Strategic goal	Core metrics
SDG 9	Innovation	Encourage the development of new technologies and solutions in the financial sector that benefit municipalities	Outside-in perspective: • Identify users' needs with regard to the development of new technologies and solutions in the financial sector. (What technologies would be necessary to improve innovation within municipality?) Inside-out perspective: • Number of new financial technologies and solutions introduced in the municipality. • Growth in the municipality's reputation as an innovation hub in the financial sector. Inside-in perspective: • Number of new technologies or solutions developed within the financial sector. Volume of transactions processed using new payment solutions
SDG 10	Financial inclusion	Enable access to basic banking services for unbanked and underbanked populations	Outside-in perspective: • Measuring the needs of unbanked and underbanked populations. (What services do you need to gain access to basic banking services?) Inside-out perspective: • Improvement in overall financial inclusion of municipality residents. • Reduction in reliance on informal financial services, leading to better financial regulation within the municipality. Inside-in perspective: • Increase in the number of unbanked and underbanked users accessing basic banking services through the platform. • Reduction in the percentage of unbanked and underbanked populations in the target region or country. • Percentage increase in financial products and services used by underserved populations. • Customer satisfaction rates among underserved populations.

Targeted SDGs

Fig. 4.7 SDG 1

SDG 1—No Poverty: Fintechs offering instant payments and cross-border transactions can help reduce poverty by lowering transaction fees and providing more accessible financial services for underserved populations (Fig. 4.7).

Fig. 4.8 SDG 8

SDG 8—Decent Work and Economic Growth: Improved remittance services can support economic growth by facilitating the flow of funds to and from developing countries, enabling individuals to invest in businesses, education, and healthcare (Fig. 4.8).

Fig. 4.9 SDG 9

SDG 9—Industry, Innovation, and Infrastructure: By providing innovative payment solutions, these fintechs can promote technological advancements and contribute to building resilient infrastructure in developing regions (Fig. 4.9).

Fig. 4.10 SDG 10. Source SDGs: (United Nations, 2020)

SDG 10—Reduced Inequalities: Instant payment and cross-border transaction providers can help bridge the gap in access to financial services, promoting economic inclusion for marginalized populations and reducing income inequalities (Fig. 4.10).

2.5 Top-Down Approach

The following chapter will describe the self-developed top-down approach of the Impact Taxonomy in more detail, thereby focusing on the level of the fintech itself. Some aspects of ESG considerations have been intentionally omitted from this impact measurement framework. For instance, the categories of Toxic Waste, Water Stress, Biodiversity and Land Use, Supply Chain Labour Standards, and Product Safety and Quality, among others that would traditionally fall within an ESG rating, are not part of this top-down approach. This deliberate exclusion is due to the fact that the framework focuses solely on fintechs and does not extend to a traditional ESG rating assessment. The color spans of the following Strategic Objectives each correspond to the category they influence, i.e., Risk Management (blue), Impact (green), and Innovation (orange).

Environmental factors play a vital role in the Impact Taxonomy, ensuring that business activities across the industry align with SDGs at a global level. This is to assert further that subjects like greenhouse gas emission reductions, energy efficiency, renewable sources of energy, and green practices within office operations form part of what guides a greater focus on sustainable growth in the fintech landscape. Swiss fintechs need to define clear KPIs, including reducing carbon footprints, energy consumption, and resource utilization, in a more systematic way by directing investments towards environmentally sustainable solutions. Therefore, Swiss fintechs can systematically measure and enhance their contribution to a greener and more sustainable financial ecosystem. This approach will manage to push for corporate accountability, emphasize environmental stewardship, and support the transition to a low-carbon and efficient resource-based economy (Table 4.28).

Table 4.28 Top-down approach (environmental factors)

☐ = Risk Management ☐ = Impact ☐ = Innovation

Impact Factors	Strategic Objectives	Performance Metrics
Environmental Factors	Commitment to Greenhouse Gas Emissions Reduction	– Percentage reduction in overall corporate carbon footprint. – Proportion of investments directed toward environmentally sustainable solutions. – Increase in growth rate of green financing initiatives.
	Advancing Energy Efficiency through In-house Processes and Fintech Solutions.	– Reduction in energy consumption per unit of output within company operations. – Cumulative energy savings facilitated by our fintech solutions. – Number of partnerships forged with energy-efficient technology providers.
	Assimilation of Renewable Energy Sources into Corporate Operations	– Percentage of total energy consumption sourced from renewable resources. – Total annual investment in renewable energy infrastructure.
	Adoption of Sustainable Practices for Office Operations and Resource Management	– Quantitative reduction in office resource consumption. – Ratio of sustainable materials utilized in office operations.

Social factors are a major element of the impact taxonomy, dealing with the industry's commitment to supporting responsible growth. These form critical areas of the taxonomy with subtopics such as employment opportunities, personnel training, workplace diversity, and fair pricing, among others. The corresponding KPIs, ranging from the creation of new employment opportunities and employee participation in training programs to adherence to fair pricing practices, allow Swiss fintechs to measure and enhance their social impact consistently. Indeed, the industry will be able to play an active role in reducing social inequalities, strengthening communities, and standing for ethical business practices (Table 4.29).

Table 4.29 Top-down approach (social factors)

☐ = Risk Management ☐ = Impact ☐ = Innovation

Impact Factors	Strategic Objectives	Performance Metrics
Social Factors	Fostering Employment Opportunities through Business Expansion and Regional Collaboration	– Total number of new employment opportunities generated. – Growth in regional collaboration and partnership opportunities. – Increase in business expansion and associated economic impact.
	Execution and Enhancement of Personnel Training and Development Schemes	– Staff participation rate in training and development programs. – Improvement in employee skills or performance post-training.
	Nurturing a Diverse and Inclusive Workplace Atmosphere	– Percentage of underrepresented groups represented within the workforce. – Employee satisfaction rate related to diversity and inclusion efforts. – Ratio of diversity-related initiatives implemented and their corresponding success rate.
	Ensuring Equitable Pricing and Terms throughout the Company's Offerings	– Percentage of customers who rate the pricing and terms as equitable and transparent. – Level of adherence to regulatory pricing standards and guidelines. – Regular audits and reviews to ascertain pricing fairness and compliance.

Governance factors are a key pillar in the Impact Taxonomy for Swiss fintechs, alluding to the instillation of sound governance principles to drive responsible and sustainable growth. Governance factors include board composition, executive remuneration, data privacy, risk management, shareholder engagement, business continuity, anti-corruption, CSR reporting, and tax transparency. The taxonomy aims to set a solid framework for governance among fintech firms. Thus, associated KPIs assure that fintechs can correctly measure their governance practices and proactively remediate any potential gaps. Including these factors within the taxonomy allows for consistent impact measurement through governance across the fintech industry and supports transparency, responsibility, and ethical decision-making disclosure (Table 4.30).

Table 4.30 Top-down approach (governance factors)

□ = Risk Management □ = Impact □ = Innovation

Impact Factors	Strategic Objectives	Performance Metrics
Governance Factors	Reinforcing Board Composition and Efficiency	– Ratio of diverse board members representing various skills, experiences, and backgrounds. – Board effectiveness score, as evaluated through a rigorous annual assessment.
	Aligning Executive Remuneration with Company Performance and Stakeholder Interests	– Correlation coefficient between executive compensation and company performance. – Percentage of executive remuneration tied to stakeholder satisfaction and long-term value creation. – Adoption of a transparent and accountable executive remuneration policy.
	Upholding Robust Data Privacy and Security Standards	– Number of data breaches or incidents reported and their severity. – Adherence to data privacy regulations and established security frameworks.
	Establishing Comprehensive Risk Management Frameworks and Procedures	– Effectiveness of risk identification, assessment, and mitigation measures. – Number of risk-related incidents and their impact on company operations.
	Strengthening Shareholder Rights and Encouraging Active Involvement	– Percentage of shareholders actively participating in company matters and decision-making. – Number of shareholder proposals implemented to enhance company governance.
	Integrating Regulatory Compliance Policies within Company Operations	– Percentage of successful regulatory audits conducted on a regular basis. – Implementation rate of corrective measures to address compliance gaps.
	Formulating Business Continuity Strategies for Long-term Resilience	– Number of critical business processes with comprehensive continuity plans. – Frequency and effectiveness of business continuity exercises and simulations.
	Instituting Anti-corruption and Anti-bribery Policies and Oversight Mechanisms	– Number of reported anti-corruption or anti-bribery incidents and their subsequent resolution. – Effectiveness of monitoring and oversight mechanisms in identifying potential risks.
	Providing Transparent and Comprehensive Corporate Social Responsibility Reporting	– Percentage of adherence to international CSR reporting standards and guidelines. – Total number of external audits conducted to validate CSR report accuracy. – Stakeholder satisfaction score related to CSR transparency and comprehensiveness.
	Demonstrating Dedication to Tax Transparency and Ethical Practices	– Percentage of compliance with international tax regulations and reporting requirements. – Frequency and outcomes of internal and external tax audits.

Economic factors, which relate to economic growth and general welfare, form another part of the Impact Taxonomy. Subtopics like economic expansion, the development of local communities, market competition, innovation, and financial stability underline significant impacts that the fintech industry can have on society. Furthermore, the related KPIs help to quantify these businesses' contribution to the initiatives in making developments in economic development, fostering market competition, and promoting financial resilience within both fintech and firms across the entire industry. This ultimately helps Swiss fintechs measure their progress in creating sustainable, far-reaching benefits for stakeholders and the broader economy (Table 4.31).

Table 4.31 Top-down approach (economic factors)

□ = Risk Management □ = Impact □ = Innovation

Impact Factors	Strategic Objectives	Performance Metrics
Economic Factors	Contributing to Economic Expansion and Local Community Advancement	– Amount invested in local community development initiatives and projects. – Percentage increase in regional economic growth attributed to company's presence.
	Cultivating Market Competition and Inspiring Innovation in the Fintech Sector	– Percentage growth in market share as a result of innovative product and service offerings. – Number of patents filed for proprietary technologies and solutions.
	Fortifying Financial Stability and Resilience within the Company and Industry	– Company's financial stability score as per industry benchmarking. – Growth in capital reserves to support financial resilience.

The addition of technological factors to the Impact Taxonomy serves to underline the significance of embracing technological innovation and maintaining robust digital infrastructures within the industry. By addressing subtopics such as resource allocation for Research and Development (R&D), digital security, and the adoption of new technologies, the taxonomy emphasizes the vital role that cutting-edge solutions play in the success and resilience of fintech businesses. The corresponding KPIs enable the evaluation of R&D outputs, efficiency in cybersecurity, and competitive advantage from using technology adoption. This focus on technological factors helps Swiss fintechs to consistently assess and enhance their capabilities, ultimately driving long-term growth and industry leadership (Table 4.32).

Table 4.32 Top-down approach (technological factors)

□ = Risk Management □ = Impact □ = Innovation

Impact Factors	Strategic Objectives	Performance Metrics
Technological Factors	Allocating Resources to Technological Advancements and R&D for Superior Service Provision	– Number of breakthrough technologies or solutions resulting from R&D investments. – Number of patents filed or granted.
	Safeguarding Digital Infrastructure and Security Excellence	– Number of digital infrastructure vulnerabilities identified and resolved. – Adoption of industry-standard cybersecurity certifications and best practices.
	Adopting Emerging Technologies to Gain a Competitive Edge	– Number of emerging technology implementations within company operations. – Increase in competitive advantage and market positioning due to technology adoption.

Regulatory factors constitute a crucial aspect of the Impact Taxonomy emphasizing the importance of agility in adapting to regulatory changes, active collaboration with regulatory bodies, and adherence to industry standards. By factoring in regulatory factors, the taxonomy will provide a consistent means for fintechs to benchmark their preparedness, responsiveness, and engagement with regulatory authorities. Swiss fintechs can ensure compliance, minimize risks, and maintain excellence in the provision of services by analyzing KPIs such as time taken to implement any introduced changes in regulations, collaborative initiatives with the regulatory stakeholders, and conformity to the industry standards (Table 4.33).

Table 4.33 Top-down approach (regulatory factors)

□ = Risk Management □ = Impact □ = Innovation

Impact Factors	Strategic Objectives	Performance Metrics
Regulatory Factors	Exhibiting Flexibility in Response to Regulatory Changes and Shifting Demands	– Average time taken to adapt and implement regulatory changes within the company. – Effectiveness in anticipating and adapting to market demand fluctuations.
	Cooperating with Regulatory Bodies to Influence Industry Directives	– Number of collaborative initiatives with regulatory bodies. – Proactive engagement with regulatory stakeholders to promote the company's interests.
	Adhering to Industry Standards and Best Practices to Guarantee Excellence	– Percentage of company processes conforming to recognized industry standards and best practices. – Improvement in operational efficiency and customer satisfaction as a result of adherence to best practices.

The integration and collaboration factors are considered an integral part of the Impact Taxonomy since they underline the need for strategic relationship development and encourage cross-sector partnership. Adopting these factors into the taxonomy will bring about a standardized measurement approach to valuing the impact created by fintechs in fostering a cooperative ecosystem underpinning shared value and bringing about innovation. By assessing relevant KPIs, such as the growth in strategic partnerships, stakeholder satisfaction levels, and the financial benefits derived from cross-sector collaborations, Swiss fintechs can develop a holistic understanding of their role in shaping a resilient, interconnected and resourceful industry landscape. This ultimately increases the capacity of the fintech sector to adapt, innovate, and thrive in line with evolving market dynamics (Table 4.34).

Table 4.34 Top-down approach (integration and collaboration factors)

□ = Risk Management □ = Impact □ = Innovation

Impact Factors	Strategic Objectives	Performance Metrics
Integration and Collaboration Factors	Fostering Relationships and Cultivating a Robust Network of Stakeholders	– Growth in the number of strategic partnerships and alliances established within the industry. – Increase in stakeholder satisfaction, measured through regular surveys and assessments.
	Promoting Cross-sector Collaboration and Synergy for Mutual Advantage	– Number of cross-sector partnerships established to drive innovation and shared value. – Increase in revenue or market presence attributable to cross-sector collaborations.

3 Quantitative Survey Analysis

The subsequent section will be dedicated to a comprehensive and systematic examination of the quantitative survey. Primarily, an evaluation of the sociodemographic data will be conducted, followed by an in-depth exploration of the deviation pertaining to both the pre-assessment and KPI-assessment as evidenced by the survey participants. Subsequent to these evaluations, the focus will shift towards the assessment of identified Impact Themes and Impact Factors. Additionally, particular emphasis will be allocated to the examination of the top KPIs. The latter part of the section will concentrate on conducting a frequency analysis, utilizing both the bottom-up and top-down approaches. Moreover, an analysis will ascertain the extent of the so-called "leapfrogging" phenomenon of fintechs with regard to traditional banks. Thereafter, the hypotheses previously proposed will undergo rigorous validation, which will be supplemented by a Backwards Stepwise Regression Analysis to further refine the understanding and to validate the correlations deduced from the data.

In general, the email distribution of the survey yielded a total of 69 impressions. Among these impressions, 57 fintechs commenced the completion of the quantitative survey and ultimately 21 participants successfully concluded the entire survey. Consequently, the termination rate stands at 30.43%.

3.1 Sociodemographic Data Analysis

The analysis of sociodemographic attributes extracted from the survey participants illuminates a geographic distribution that is predominantly focused on the financial hubs of Switzerland. The majority of fintech firms that have partaken in the survey are established in the canton of Zurich, representing 26 participants. This is followed by the canton of Zug, with 14 participants and then the canton of Schwyz, hosting 4 participants. This regional share aligns well with the anticipations based on existing knowledge about the fintech landscape in Switzerland (Fig. 4.11).

With regard to the role of the participants of the survey, it can be derived from the observed results that most of them were CEOs, Founders / Co-Founders of their respective fintechs. However, it has to be mentioned that 12 respondents selected the option labeled "Other" as an alternative. On further examination, it was found that this choice predominantly comprised those who described themselves as "ESG / Impact Experts" alongside four other respondents. Among others, responses identifying roles as "Head of Business Development", "Chief Commercial Officer", "Managing Director", "Head Business Development", "Customer Relations", "Analyst", "Advisor", and "Sales Manager" (Fig. 4.12).

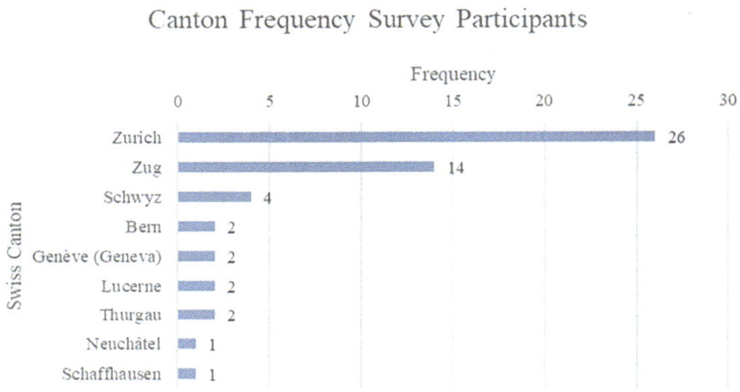

Fig. 4.11 Canton frequency survey participants. © Dr. Karen Wendt and Mathias Hauser, 2024

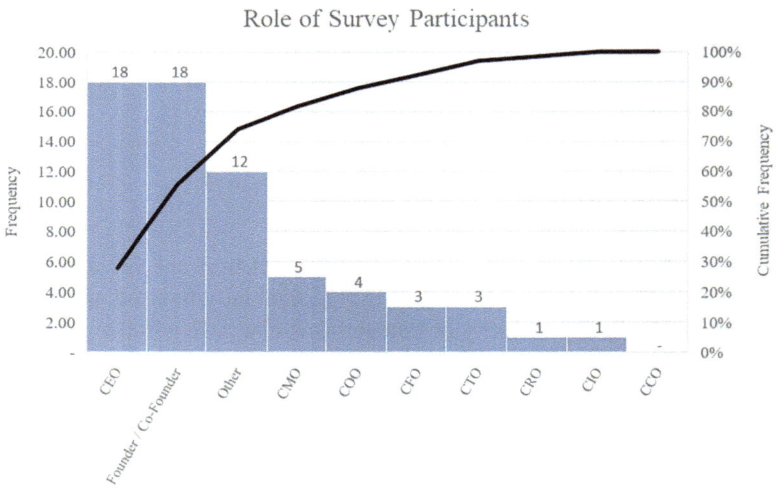

Fig. 4.12 Role of survey participants. © Dr. Karen Wendt and Mathias Hauser, 2024

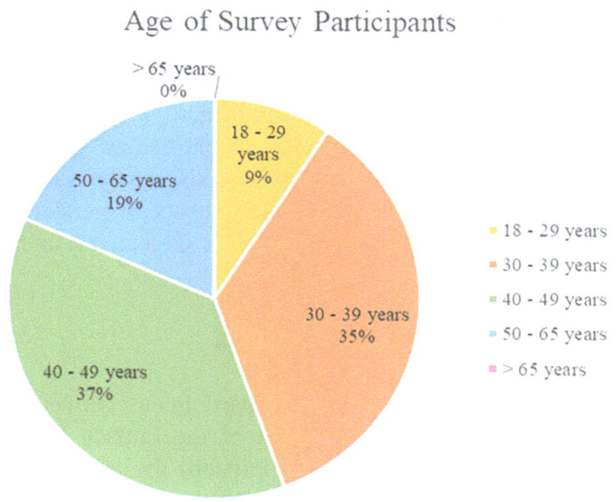

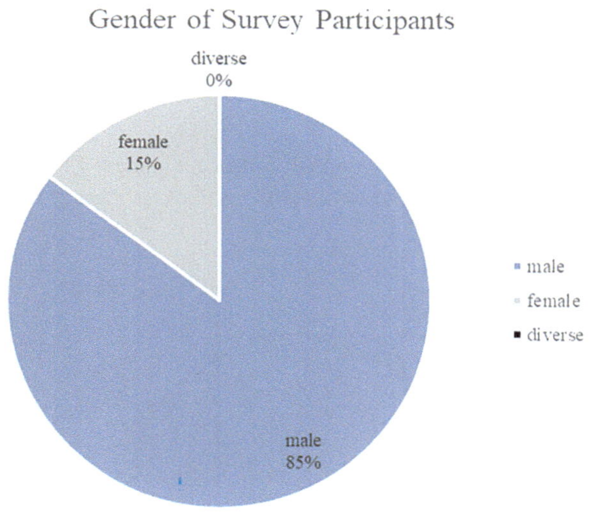

Fig. 4.13 (**a**) Age of survey participants. (**b**) Gender of survey participants. © Dr. Karen Wendt and Mathias Hauser, 2024

On the aspect of the age demography of the survey participants, there was broad representation of different age groups according to the data presented in Fig. 4.13. The "40–49 years" age group is the most significant proportion of the participants in the survey and is represented by 37% of the total. This is closely followed by the group of ages presented as "30–39 years", which is 35% of the total participants who participated in the survey. Another 19% of the overall participants were in the age group category "50–65 years". The youngest survey participants, under the label "18–29 years", accounted for a substantial 9% of the overall participants in the survey. Although there has been a lack of inputs from older participants of the study, who belong to the age group "> 65 years". These key findings emphasize the variety of participation across multiple age groups and therefore offer a range of views and experiences within the data set.

In relation to the gender of the survey participants, 85% identified as "males", whereas 15% identified as "females", and none identified as "diverse", as shown in Fig. 4.13. This distribution hinders the comprehensive analysis of the dataset, particularly with regard to assessing the potential impact of gender as a significant variable for the identified Impact Themes, Strategic Objectives, and KPIs.

3.2 Impact Themes & Factors Analysis

In order to analyze the deviations of survey participants between the initial pre-assessment compared to the KPI-assessment of the Impact Themes (bottom-up approach) and Impact Factors (top-down approach) the average scoring of each category has been represented in the radar map, shown in Figs. 4.14 and 4.15. It can be asserted from the data that the categories "Innovation", "Financial Resilience", "Financial Inclusion", and "Sustainability" have scored higher during the Pre-Assessment. Whereas, the categories "Gender Equality", "Economic Growth",

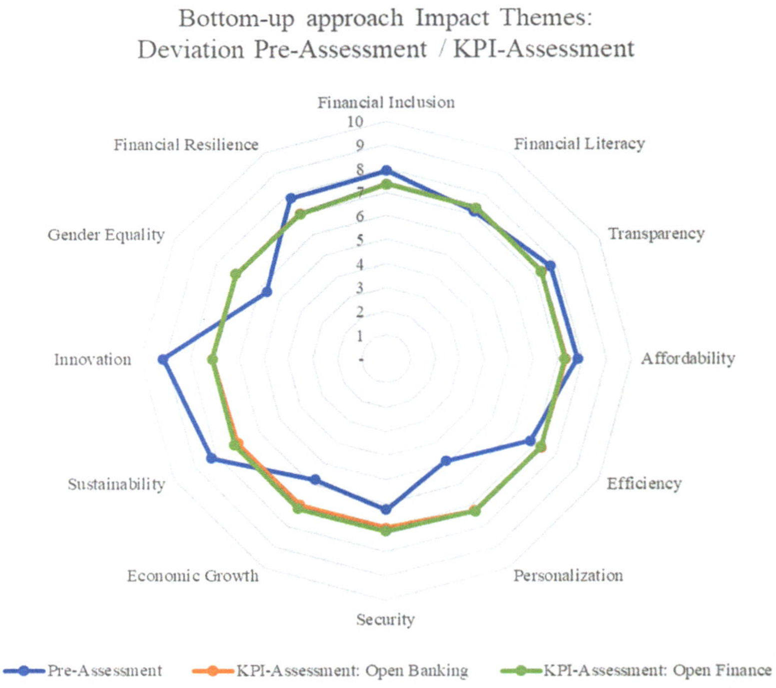

Fig. 4.14 Bottom-up approach impact themes deviation pre-assessment / KPI-assessment. © Dr. Karen Wendt and Mathias Hauser, 2024

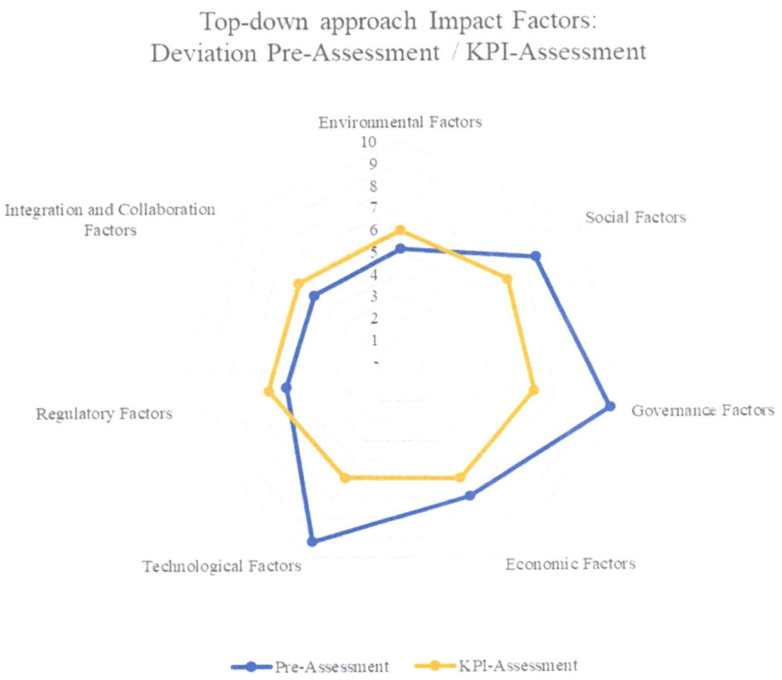

Fig. 4.15 Top-down approach impact factors deviation pre-assessment / KPI-assessment. © Dr. Karen Wendt and Mathias Hauser, 2024

"Security", "Personalization", and "Efficiency" have scored higher during the KPI-Assessment for the bottom-up approach.

Regarding the top-down approach, the data reveals that the categories "Social Factors", "Governance Factors", "Economic Factors", and "Technological Factors" have scored higher during the initial pre-assessment of the Impact Factors. Conversely, the categories "Regulatory Factors", "Integration and Collaboration Factors" as well as "Environmental Factors" obtained a slightly higher score during the KPI-assessment.

3.3 Key Performance Indicators Analysis

In order to gain a deeper insight into the preferences of the survey participants, Table 4.35 presents the Open Banking KPIs that obtained the highest average scores

Table 4.35 Top 10 KPIs description Open Banking (bottom-up approach). © Dr. Karen Wendt and Mathias Hauser, 2024

Category	KPI-Description	Score
Sustainability	Reduction in the municipality's risk of extreme weather threats	8.90
Innovation	Identify the user's needs with regard to the development of new technologies and solutions in the financial sector. (What technologies would be necessary to improve innovation within municipality?)	8.90
Sustainability	Reduction in the municipality's carbon footprint due to the adoption of digital banking services	8.70
Transparency	Reduction in hidden fees or charges experienced by users	8.67
Innovation	Growth in the municipality's reputation as an innovation hub in the financial sector	8.60
Efficiency	Increase in cross-border money transfers and associated time and cost savings within the municipality	8.56
Affordability	Savings in transaction fees for residents, compared to traditional banking services	8.50
Innovation	Number of new financial technologies and solutions introduced in the municipality	8.50
Innovation	Number of new technologies or solutions developed within the financial sector	8.44
Transparency	Reduction in transaction fees and increased pricing transparency for municipality residents	8.42

through the bottom-up approach. The data reveals that among the Top 10 KPIs for Open Banking, the Impact Theme "Innovation" is featured four times, followed by "Sustainability" and "Transparency" with two occurrences each. Furthermore, "Efficiency" is represented once, while "Affordability" is also represented once.

For Open Banking fintechs a high-impact generation is allocated in areas such as environmental sustainability, user-centered technology development, cost transparency, and fostering an innovative ecosystem within municipalities. Environmental impact is evident in the reduction of the municipality's carbon footprint due to the adoption of digital banking services and lessened risk of extreme weather threats. This indicates that Swiss fintechs in the dataset place a high value on impact generation with regard to climate change mitigation efforts through digitization strategies. Additionally, Swiss fintechs place considerable emphasis on the generation of impact by prioritizing user requirements and the advancement of emerging technologies in the financial sector. This demonstrates their dedication to fostering substantial positive outcomes through their contributions to financial innovation, inclusivity, and user-centric advancements within the realm of finance. Moreover, Swiss fintechs place a high emphasis on the development of new technologies in the financial sector, which implies that they allocate a high-impact generation by contributions to financial innovation, inclusivity, and user-centered innovation within the financial sector. The KPIs regarding the reduction in hidden fees, transaction fees, and the increase in pricing transparency reflect a high-impact generation based on fairness and transparency. Therefore, reducing the costs of financial services and making them more affordable and accessible to residents contributes to economic inclusivity and equity. Besides that, the fintechs allocated a high-impact generation towards cross-border money transfers and associated time and cost savings within the municipality. Finally, the emphasis on growing the municipality's reputation as an innovation hub in the financial sector, combined with the number of new financial technologies and solutions introduced, indicates a substantial impact generation by creating a vibrant, forward-thinking ecosystem. In addition to the Top 10 KPIs, it can be observed from the underlying dataset that a majority of the KPIs that aim to measure user satisfaction within the Impact Themes tend to yield lower scores compared to other KPIs within the same Impact Theme. This observation leads to the conclusion that user satisfaction, in and of itself, does not constitute the primary driver of impact generation.

In the context of Open Finance, Table 4.36 illustrates that the Top 10 KPIs predominantly revolve around the Impact Themes of "Sustainability" and "Innovation",

Table 4.36 Top 10 KPIs description Open Finance (bottom-up approach). © Dr. Karen Wendt and Mathias Hauser, 2024

Category	KPI-Description	Score
Sustainability	Improved long-term financial and environmental outcomes for municipalities	9.09
Innovation	Improvement in data-driven decision-making capabilities for municipalities using the technology platforms	9.09
Sustainability	Determine the users' need to drive capital towards sustainable and responsible investments. (How can the fintech drive capital towards sustainable and responsible investments and support municipalities?)	8.98
Sustainability	Increase in AuM allocated to sustainable and responsible investments	8.98
Efficiency	Improvement of the onboarding duration for new users on the investment platform	8.86
Sustainability	Enhanced reputation of municipalities as responsible investors	8.86
Innovation	Enhanced capacity for scalability and growth in municipal operations, enabled by technology-driven platforms	8.86
Innovation	Determine the users' need to develop platforms that leverage emerging technologies. (How can fintechs create innovative financial solutions for municipalities?)	8.75
Innovation	Higher rate of innovation in municipal services and programs as a result of leveraging emerging technologies	8.75
Financial resilience	Enhanced long-term financial planning and performance for municipalities	8.75

each with four occurrences. Subsequently, "Efficiency" and "Financial Resilience" are represented once each among the Top 10 KPIs. For Open Finance fintechs high-impact generation is attributed to areas such as long-term financial and environmental outcomes, data-driven decision-making, sustainable investments, user onboarding efficiency, innovation, and scalability. A focus on improved financial and environmental outcomes indicates these fintechs allocate significant impact generation towards driving sustainable prosperity within municipalities. Therefore, leveraging platforms to improve data-driven decision-making capabilities and promoting more informed, efficient, and effective operational and investment decisions within municipalities are considered highly impactful. Moreover, the emphasis on understanding user needs in directing capital towards sustainable and responsible investments reveals a conscious effort by Swiss fintechs to support municipalities' ESG goals. This commitment is further underscored by the emphasis on increasing AuM allocated to such investments. Moreover, the focus is directed towards generating significant impact in terms of improving user onboarding duration, which reflects their commitment to user experience, potentially increasing accessibility and democratization of asset management solutions. The emphasis on enhancing the reputation of municipalities as responsible investors and the capacity for scalability and growth in their operations indicates a broader, transformative impact on the municipalities' financial operations and reputation. Furthermore, the Top 10 KPIs reflect a commitment to innovation and technology adoption, with KPIs focusing on user needs to develop platforms leveraging emerging technologies. This drive contributes to a higher rate of innovation in municipal services and programs, positioning municipalities at the forefront of technological advancement in finance. Finally, the enhanced long-term financial planning and performance for municipalities indicates these fintechs' contributions to a stable and sustainable financial future for these regions. Apart from the Top 10 KPIs, it is evident that a significant proportion of the KPIs targeting user satisfaction within the underlying Impact Themes generally produce lower scores when compared to other KPIs in the same Impact Theme. This finding ultimately suggests that user satisfaction, on its own, does not serve as the principal catalyst for generating impact.

With regard to the top-down approach, based on Table 4.37, it can be identified that the Impact Factor "Governance Factors" has found the highest number of

Table 4.37 Top 10 KPIs description top-down approach

Category	KPI-Description	Score
Governance factors	Board effectiveness score, as evaluated through a rigorous annual assessment	8.69
Governance factors	Percentage of executive remuneration tied to stakeholder satisfaction and long-term value creation	8.57
Governance factors	Effectiveness of risk identification, assessment, and mitigation measures	8.13
Governance factors	Number of risk-related incidents and their impact on company operations	8.13
Governance factors	Ratio of diverse board members representing various skills, experiences, and backgrounds	7.98
Environmental factors	Proportion of investments directed toward environmentally sustainable solutions	7.95
Environmental factors	Percentage reduction in overall corporate carbon footprint	7.84
Social factors	Improvement in employee skills or performance post-training	7.74
Social factors	Total number of new employment opportunities generated	7.62
Environmental factors	Reduction in energy consumption per unit of output within company operations	7.61

representations, as mentioned five times among the Top 10 KPIs. Following this, "Environmental Factors" are represented three times, while "Social Factors" are represented twice. The highlighted emphasis on governance components may suggest that Swiss fintechs perceive a powerful effect emanating from a level of good governance exercised by fintechs. This perspective is possibly influenced by the COVID-19 pandemic—the empirical results exhibit a marked tendency toward risk management. The findings using the top-down approach highlight that the Swiss fintech sector places effective governance, environmental sustainability, and employee development as high-impact generation areas. High-impact generation is also attributed to the redefined traditional governance structures by the emphasis that Swiss fintechs place on board effectiveness and executive remuneration tied to stakeholder satisfaction and long-term value creation. This leads to an improved decision-making process and transparency, thus increasing stakeholders' trust, which further contributes to generating a healthier ecosystem for all participants. The emphasis on risk management, demonstrated by the prioritization of minimizing incidents of risks, indicates an industry that is serious about resilience and stability. Swiss fintechs strongly contribute to creating an impact by being anticipatory in the operation of risks and their mitigation, thereby ensuring the overall stability of the Swiss financial system for accommodating businesses and protecting their stakeholders. This is vital for closer collaboration with the industry and encouragement toward inclusivity and continuous learning. Even more importantly, the firm's emphasis on diversity within its board and improvement in skills and commitment by employees even after training testifies to an industry that cherishes diverse perspectives and believes in harnessing its human capital for future success. This leads to the generation of a broader range of ideas and solutions, driving innovation while ensuring opportunities for all and contributing to social equality. In terms of environmental sustainability, the industry's emphasis on KPIs related to environmentally sustainable investments, reductions in carbon footprint, and energy efficiency indicates a significant allocation of impact creation towards combating climate change. Lastly, the industry's emphasis on creating new employment opportunities underlines the significant socio-economic impact that fintechs can have.

3.4 Frequency Analysis

The frequency analysis for the bottom-up approach (Open Banking) displays aggregations of the average scoring values for each Impact Theme based on the selected answers for each KPI within the Impact Theme. When looking at the aggregate data, as shown in Fig. 4.16, the data suggests that the aggregated frequency graph of the Impact Themes "Innovation" and "Sustainability indicates a characteristic of an exponential growth pattern. This means that only a marginal number, if any, of the KPIs have been classified as "Highly Irrelevant", with a higher prevalence for the "Relevant" category and, most prominently, the "Highly Relevant" category. Moreover, the frequency analysis also shows a proclivity towards the classification as "Relevant" demonstrating a linear cumulative progression for the Impact Themes

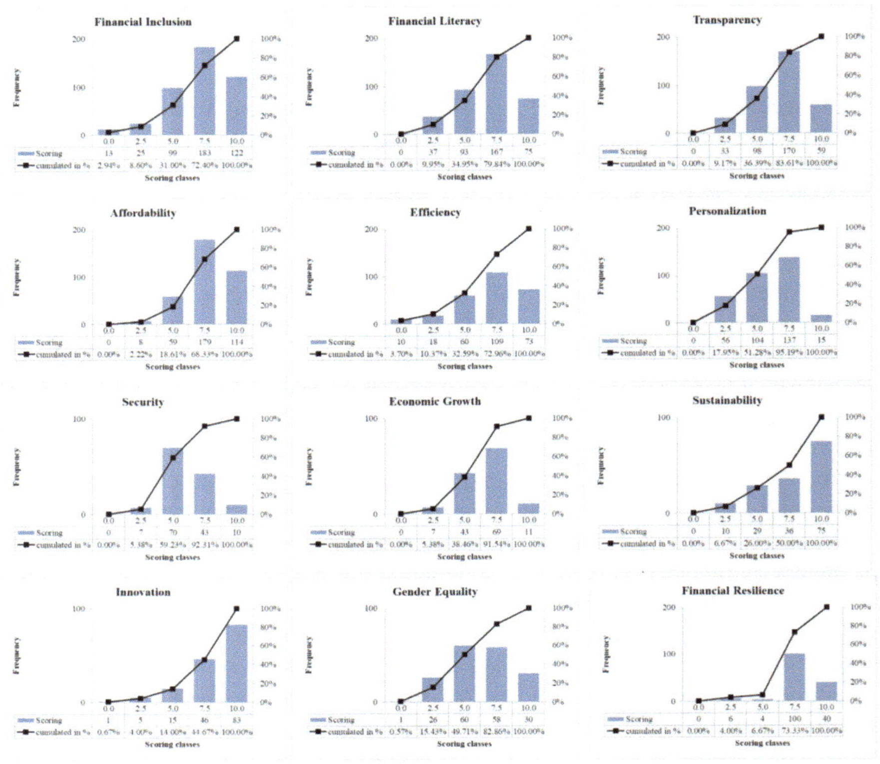

Fig. 4.16 Frequency analysis bottom-up approach Open Banking. © Dr. Karen Wendt and Mathias Hauser, 2024

"Financial Inclusion", "Financial Literacy", "Transparency", "Affordability", and "Efficiency". It is also noteworthy that in the Impact Themes of "Economic Growth" and "Personalization", the cumulative frequency curve shows a much flatter trend at the higher percentiles. In fact, this is due to the lower prevalence for the option "Highly Relevant". In the case of the Impact Theme "Security" it is worth noting that the peak of the frequency distribution lies within the "Somewhat Relevant" category, again showing a weaker total contribution to the impact in that dimension. On the other hand, for the Impact Theme "Gender Equality" the frequency distribution peaks within the "Somewhat Relevant" and "Relevant" categorizations, therefore nearly approximating the appearance of a left-skewed normal distribution, when examining the bar chart instead of the cumulative trendline.

Upon comparison, the frequency analysis concerning Open Finance exhibits remarkable similarity to Open Banking. This parallelism is indicative of a broader trend where patterns of relevance associated with various KPIs within these sectors appear to be analogous. Such alignment may be reflective of a similar interpretation of the underlying Impact Themes for both domains. This homogeneity warrants further exploration to elucidate potential shared dynamics, paving the way for future studies. The observed consistency emphasizes the interconnectedness of these fields

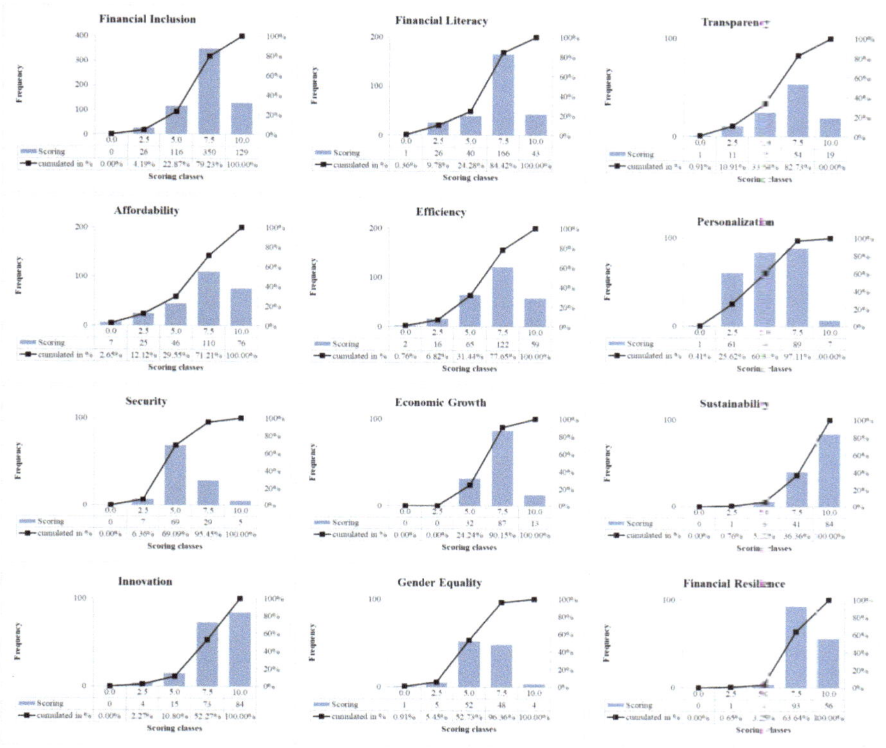

Fig. 4.17 Frequency analysis bottom-up approach Open Finance. © Dr. Karen Wendt and Mathias Hauser, 2024

and underscores the need for a unified approach to optimize their respective potential in generating positive impact (Fig. 4.17).

On scrutinizing the top-down approach, it turns out that the Impact Factors "Economic Factors", "Technological Factors", "Governance Factors", and "Regulatory Factors" follow a somewhat similar pattern. The minor response options like "Highly Irrelevant" and "Irrelevant" show hardly any frequency. The majority of the dataset tends to congregate around the "Relevant" response option, while the higher percentile "Highly Relevant" response option records a sparse frequency. In addition to this, a linear cumulative frequency trend appears from analyzing the Impact Factors of "Environmental Factors" and "Social Factors". This trend tends to suggest that a spectrum of impact generation encompasses a broader range, although the very highest percentile records a low frequency. In contrast, the Impact Factor "Integration and Collaboration Factors" shows a high frequency in the bottom quartiles, particularly within the categories "Irrelevant" and "Somewhat Relevant". It indicates that the dimension of "Integration and Collaboration Factors" might be assigned a shallow impact by fintechs (Fig. 4.18).

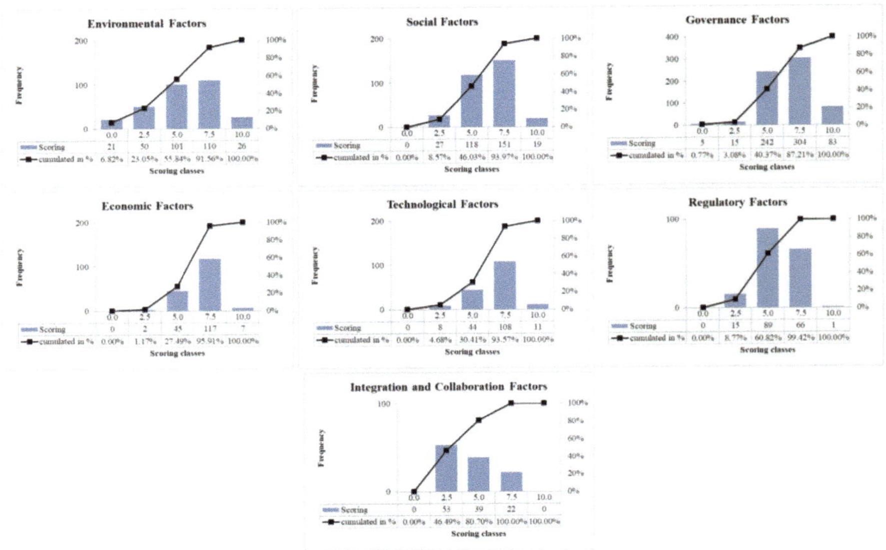

Fig. 4.18 Frequency analysis top-down approach. © Dr. Karen Wendt and Mathias Hauser, 2024

3.5 Hypothesis Testing

This chapter applies hypothesis testing to enable a comprehensive comparison and extensive interpretation of the empirical findings. The forthcoming discussion will be dedicated to the utilization of a statistical t-test for independent samples. Furthermore, it is essential to establish the robustness of the t-test in handling deviations from the assumption of a normal distribution. Accordingly, the Impact Themes identified for the bottom-up approach and the Impact Factors identified for the top-down approach were graphically displayed in a histogram with normal distribution, according to Fig. 4.19, in order to determine the robustness of the t-test. It should be noted that given the critical commonality displayed in nearly all histograms of the Impact Themes and Impact Factors, there has been a witting decision not to incorporate every such graphic illustration.

Due to the fact that the histogram, according to Fig. 4.19, does not perfectly align with the Gaussian distribution a Quantile-Quantile (Q-Q) plot analysis, according to Fig. 4.20, has been carried out, which provides a systematic and visual means of assessing if the data is normally distributed. According to Loy et al. (2016) the Q-Q plot graphically illustrates the correspondence between the observed and theoretical quantiles of the dataset (pp. 202–204). In order to prevent redundancy, the inclusion of Q-Q plots for the Impact Themes and Impact Factors within this chapter has been omitted. After conducting the Q-Q plot analysis, an approximate normal distribution of the samples based on the principles of the central limit theorem is assumed.

Consequently, the execution of the t-test yields the ensuing outcome for the bottom-up approach:

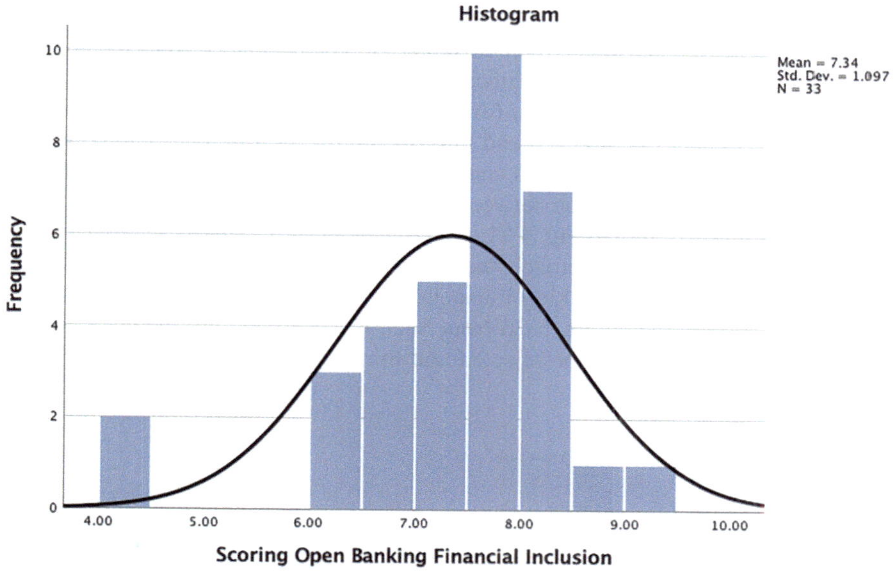

Fig. 4.19 Normal distribution histogram analysis: financial inclusion. © Dr. Karen Wendt and Mathias Hauser, 2024

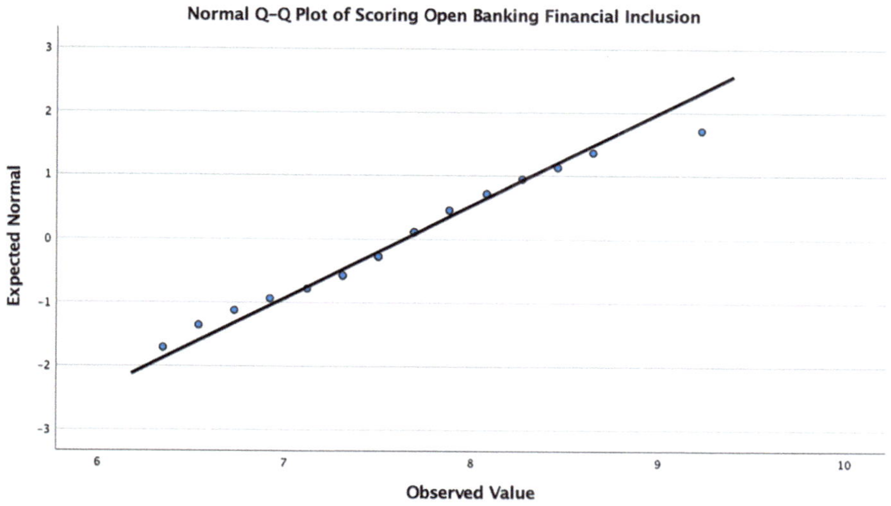

Fig. 4.20 Q-Q Plot analysis Open Banking (Financial Inclusion). © Dr. Karen Wendt and Mathias Hauser, 2024

Since the Levene test of variance equality is above the significance level of 5% in each case, variance homogeneity of the two groups (Open Banking / Open Finance) is assumed. Consequently, the pertinent outcomes are examined and evaluated herein in accordance with the specified hypotheses.

The obtained p-value from comparing the anticipated scores for "Open Banking Financial Inclusion" between Open Banking and Open Finance fintechs is 0.078. This value surpasses the predetermined significance level of 5 percent, indicating that it is not statistically significant (df(19) = 1.861, p = 0.078). Consequently, the H_0 hypotheses cannot be rejected and thus no significant difference can be identified. In conclusion, no significant deviation in the preferences of the "Open Banking Financial Inclusion" dimension between Open Banking and Open Finance fintechs can be proven. According to Fig. 4.21, the same analysis applies to all other Impact Themes for the bottom-up approach, therefore rendering the same conclusion as just described for the "Open Banking Financial Inclusion" dimension. Therefore, the formulated H_0 hypotheses Nr. 1–26 from Sect. 6.1 in Chap. 2 Hypothesis for the bottom-up approach cannot be rejected and thus no significant difference can be identified.

Independent Samples Test

		Levene's Test for Equality of Variances		t-test for Equality of Means							
						Significance				95% Confidence Interval of the Difference	
		F	Sig.	t	df	One-Sided p	Two-Sided p	Mean Difference	Std. Error Difference	Lower	Upper
Scoring Open Banking Financial Inclusion	Equal variances assumed	3.258	0.087	1.861	19	0.039	0.078	1.04143	0.55949	-0.12959	2.21245
	Equal variances not assumed			2.396	18.635	0.014	0.027	1.04143	0.43468	0.13043	1.95243
Scoring Open Banking Financial Literacy	Equal variances assumed	2.700	0.117	1.823	19	0.042	0.084	1.00643	0.55204	-0.14899	2.16185
	Equal variances not assumed			2.308	18.915	0.016	0.032	1.00643	0.43597	0.09365	1.91920
Scoring Open Banking Transparency	Equal variances assumed	2.163	0.158	1.847	19	0.040	0.080	0.97000	0.52521	-0.12927	2.06927
	Equal variances not assumed			2.267	18.922	0.018	0.035	0.97000	0.42783	0.07429	1.86571
Scoring Open Banking Affordability	Equal variances assumed	2.163	0.158	1.847	19	0.040	0.080	0.97000	0.52521	-0.12927	2.06927
	Equal variances not assumed			2.267	18.922	0.018	0.035	0.97000	0.42783	0.07429	1.86571
Scoring Open Banking Efficiency	Equal variances assumed	1.447	0.244	1.744	19	0.049	0.097	0.90429	0.51854	-0.18102	1.98959
	Equal variances not assumed			2.081	18.416	0.026	0.052	0.90429	0.43465	-0.00740	1.81597
Scoring Open Banking Personalization	Equal variances assumed	1.523	0.232	1.520	19	0.072	0.145	0.76714	0.50456	-0.28890	1.82319
	Equal variances not assumed			1.756	17.431	0.048	0.097	0.76714	0.43688	-0.15287	1.68715
Scoring Open Banking Security	Equal variances assumed	1.055	0.317	1.109	19	0.141	0.281	0.53214	0.47991	-0.47231	1.53660
	Equal variances not assumed			1.232	15.987	0.118	0.236	0.53214	0.43177	-0.38323	1.44751
Scoring Open Banking Economic Growth	Equal variances assumed	0.667	0.424	0.955	19	0.176	0.351	0.44000	0.46063	-0.52410	1.40410
	Equal variances not assumed			1.053	15.670	0.154	0.308	0.44000	0.41777	-0.44715	1.32715
Scoring Open Banking Sustainability	Equal variances assumed	0.744	0.399	0.713	19	0.242	0.484	0.31429	0.44066	-0.60802	1.23659
	Equal variances not assumed			0.788	15.746	0.221	0.442	0.31429	0.39889	-0.53242	1.16100
Scoring Open Banking Innovation	Equal variances assumed	0.778	0.389	0.671	19	0.255	0.510	0.30214	0.45003	-0.63977	1.24406
	Equal variances not assumed			0.755	16.453	0.230	0.461	0.30214	0.40008	-0.54410	1.14839
Scoring Open Banking Gender Equality	Equal variances assumed	0.871	0.362	0.879	19	0.195	0.391	0.40214	0.45766	-0.55575	1.36003
	Equal variances not assumed			1.004	17.033	0.165	0.330	0.40214	0.40069	-0.44311	1.24740
Scoring Open Banking Financial Resilience	Equal variances assumed	1.400	0.251	1.055	19	0.152	0.304	0.47714	0.45206	-0.46904	1.42332
	Equal variances not assumed			1.272	18.641	0.110	0.219	0.47714	0.37514	-0.30905	1.26334
Scoring Open Finance Financial Inclusion	Equal variances assumed	2.686	0.121	0.851	16	0.204	0.408	0.49221	0.57863	-0.73444	1.71886
	Equal variances not assumed			1.032	12.875	0.161	0.321	0.49221	0.47700	-0.53930	1.52372
Scoring Open Finance Financial Literacy	Equal variances assumed	2.722	0.118	0.927	16	0.184	0.368	0.52208	0.56309	-0.67163	1.71578
	Equal variances not assumed			1.123	12.951	0.141	0.282	0.52208	0.46476	-0.48236	1.52651
Scoring Open Finance Transparency	Equal variances assumed	2.755	0.116	0.960	16	0.176	0.352	0.53766	0.56029	-0.65010	1.72543
	Equal variances not assumed			1.163	12.927	0.133	0.266	0.53766	0.46227	-0.46158	1.53690
Scoring Open Finance Affordability	Equal variances assumed	2.755	0.116	0.960	16	0.176	0.352	0.53766	0.56029	-0.65010	1.72543
	Equal variances not assumed			1.163	12.927	0.133	0.266	0.53766	0.46227	-0.46158	1.53690
Scoring Open Finance Efficiency	Equal variances assumed	2.419	0.139	0.964	16	0.175	0.349	0.53623	0.55632	-0.64311	1.71558
	Equal variances not assumed			1.156	13.548	0.134	0.268	0.53623	0.46373	-0.46149	1.53396
Scoring Open Finance Personalization	Equal variances assumed	2.597	0.127	0.987	16	0.169	0.338	0.54740	0.55473	-0.62857	1.72338
	Equal variances not assumed			1.184	13.550	0.128	0.257	0.54740	0.46242	-0.44748	1.54229
Scoring Open Finance Security	Equal variances assumed	2.440	0.138	0.797	16	0.219	0.437	0.43636	0.54763	-0.72457	1.59729
	Equal variances not assumed			0.951	13.860	0.179	0.358	0.43636	0.45899	-0.54900	1.42172
Scoring Open Finance Economic Growth	Equal variances assumed	2.480	0.135	0.832	16	0.209	0.418	0.45000	0.54089	-0.69663	1.59663
	Equal variances not assumed			1.001	13.397	0.167	0.335	0.45000	0.44971	-0.51863	1.41863
Scoring Open Finance Sustainability	Equal variances assumed	2.198	0.158	0.897	16	0.191	0.383	0.47519	0.52948	-0.64724	1.59763
	Equal variances not assumed			1.074	13.708	0.151	0.301	0.47519	0.44258	-0.47594	1.42633
Scoring Open Finance Innovation	Equal variances assumed	1.727	0.207	0.908	16	0.189	0.377	0.48377	0.53294	-0.64601	1.61354
	Equal variances not assumed			1.078	14.106	0.150	0.299	0.48377	0.44868	-0.47788	1.44541
Scoring Open Finance Gender Equality	Equal variances assumed	1.727	0.207	0.908	16	0.189	0.377	0.48377	0.53294	-0.64601	1.61354
	Equal variances not assumed			1.078	14.106	0.150	0.299	0.48377	0.44868	-0.47788	1.44541
Scoring Open Finance Financial Resilience	Equal variances assumed	1.637	0.219	0.765	16	0.228	0.455	0.40675	0.53173	-0.72045	1.53396
	Equal variances not assumed			0.909	14.063	0.189	0.378	0.40675	0.44730	-0.55221	1.36572

Fig. 4.21 Independent t-test for the bottom-up approach. © Dr. Karen Wendt and Mathias Hauser, 2024

Exemplary representation of the defined H_0 hypotheses for the "Open Banking Financial Inclusion" dimension to avoid duplication (Fig. 4.22):

Moreover, the execution of the t-test yields the ensuing outcome for the top-down approach:

Given that the Levene test of variance equality exceeds the 5% significance level for both groups (Open Banking / Open Finance), it is assumed that the variance is homogeneous in the test. Hence, the relevant results are analyzed and assessed in this context based on the predetermined hypotheses.

The obtained p-value from comparing the anticipated scores for "Environmental Factors" between Open Banking and Open Finance fintechs is 0.740. This value surpasses the predetermined significance level of 5 percent, indicating that it is not statistically significant (df(15) = 0.338, p = 0.740). Consequently, the H_0 hypotheses cannot be rejected and thus no significant difference can be identified. In conclusion, no significant deviation in the preferences of the "Environmental Factors" dimension between Open Banking and Open Finance fintechs can be proven. According to Fig. 4.23, the same analysis applies to all other Impact Factors for the top-down approach, therefore rendering the same conclusion as just described for the "Environmental Factors" dimension. Therefore, the formulated H_0 hypotheses Nr. 27–40 from Sect. 6.1 in Chap. 2 Hypothesis for the top-down approach cannot be rejected and thus no significant difference can be identified (Fig. 4.24).

Financial Inclusion:		
1	H_0:	Open Banking and Open Finance fintechs have the same expected scoring values for the "Financial Inclusion" dimension and are therefore considered homogeneous in their sustainability preferences.
2	H_A:	Open Banking and Open Finance fintechs do not have the same expected scoring values according to the "Financial Inclusion" dimension and are therefore considered to be heterogeneous in their sustainability preferences.

Fig. 4.22 Hypotheses testing bottom-up approach financial inclusion

Independent Samples Test

		Levene's Test for Equality of Variances		t-test for Equality of Means							
						Significance				95% Confidence Interval of the Difference	
		F	Sig.	t	df	One-Sided p	Two-Sided p	Mean Difference	Std. Error Difference	Lower	Upper
Scoring Environmental Factors	Equal variances assumed	0.972	0.340	0.338	15	0.370	0.740	0.13143	0.38876	-0.69719	0.96005
	Equal variances not assumed			0.360	14.983	0.362	0.724	0.13143	0.36514	-0.64693	0.90979
Scoring Social Factors	Equal variances assumed	2.860	0.111	0.394	15	0.350	0.699	0.13743	0.34889	-0.60621	0.88106
	Equal variances not assumed			0.428	14.886	0.337	0.675	0.13743	0.32122	-0.54770	0.82256
Scoring Governance Factors	Equal variances assumed	2.115	0.166	0.528	15	0.303	0.605	0.17986	0.34085	-0.54665	0.90636
	Equal variances not assumed			0.574	14.874	0.287	0.575	0.17986	0.31361	-0.48908	0.84879
Scoring Econonmic Factors	Equal variances assumed	0.696	0.417	0.277	15	0.393	0.786	0.09314	0.33642	-0.62393	0.81021
	Equal variances not assumed			0.294	14.971	0.386	0.773	0.09314	0.31654	-0.58167	0.76795
Scoring Technological Factors	Equal variances assumed	0.151	0.703	0.019	15	0.492	0.985	0.00700	0.36589	-0.77287	0.78687
	Equal variances not assumed			0.020	14.414	0.492	0.984	0.00700	0.35379	-0.74977	0.76377
Scoring Regulatory Factors	Equal variances assumed	0.667	0.427	-0.656	15	0.261	0.522	-0.22700	0.34605	-0.96458	0.51058
	Equal variances not assumed			-0.679	14.445	0.254	0.508	-0.22700	0.33428	-0.94189	0.48789
Scoring Integration and Collaboration Factors	Equal variances assumed	0.365	0.555	-0.828	15	0.210	0.421	-0.29671	0.35829	-1.06039	0.46696
	Equal variances not assumed			-0.867	14.755	0.200	0.400	-0.29671	0.34205	-1.02684	0.43341

Fig. 4.23 Independent t-test for the top-down approach. © Dr. Karen Wendt and Mathias Hauser, 2024

Environmental Factors:		
27	H_0:	Open Banking and Open Finance fintechs have the same expected scoring values for the "Environmental Factors" dimension and are therefore considered homogeneous in their sustainability preferences.
28	H_A:	Open Banking and Open Finance fintechs do not have the same expected scoring values according to the "Environmental Factors" dimension and are therefore considered to be heterogeneous in their sustainability preferences.

Fig. 4.24 Hypotheses testing top-down approach environmental factors

3.6 Backward Stepwise Regression

The comprehensive examination of the nominal and ordinal scaled sociodemographic variables delineated within this study, including role, canton, gender, age, and sustainability-related groups, are tested for significance on the basis of their scalability using several backward stepwise regressions in a sequential algorithm. The adoption of such a sequential process in this research method assists in the systematic elimination of statistically insignificant predictors and thereby promotes a robust and efficacious model.

Due to the fact that several socio-demographic factors were retrieved as separate variables during the quantitative survey, it was imperative to aggregate such characteristics to one factor. This involves combining individual attributes such as role and sustainability-related groups for analytical purposes. The procedure of Backwards Stepwise Regression has been meticulously applied to all Impact Themes stemming from the bottom-up approach, as well as to all Impact Factors originating from the top-down approach. To circumvent repetition and maintain brevity, a comprehensive description of the Backwards Stepwise Regression methodology is offered only in the context of the "Open Banking Financial Inclusion" variable. It should be noted that the same analytical methodology is uniformly applied across all other Impact Themes and Impact Factors (Fig. 4.25).

For the Bottom-Up Approach in Open Banking, the Data Elucidates Several Pertinent Relationships

The variable "Age" emerges as a critical determinant, significantly impacting "Financial Inclusion", "Financial Literacy", "Transparency", "Affordability", and "Sustainability". This underscores the crucial role of demographic profiles in influencing these aspects of Open Banking. The geographical variable "Canton" manifests a notable influence on "Innovation". This suggests that regional factors might play a pivotal role in shaping innovation within the Open Banking domain. Both "Age" and "Canton" jointly exert significant effects on "Gender Equality" and "Financial Resilience" in Open Banking. The results intimate that an interplay between demographic and regional factors could be integral to these facets. However, for "Efficiency", "Personalization", "Security", and "Economic Growth" within Open Banking, no significant influence can be detected.

For the Bottom-Up Approach in Open Finance, the Data Reveals no Significant Influence

Turning the attention to Open Finance within the bottom-up approach, the regression analysis yields no significant influence on any of the assessed aspects:

Coefficients[a]

Model		Unstandardized Coefficients B	Unstandardized Coefficients Std. Error	Standardized Coefficients Beta	t	Sig.
1	(Constant)	5.902	1.291		4.573	<0.001
	Role	0.035	0.062	0.112	0.571	0.573
	Canton	0.054	0.038	0.248	1.431	0.164
	Gender	-0.517	0.467	-0.196	-1.107	0.278
	Age	0.502	0.238	0.391	2.111	0.044
	Sustainability-related groups	-0.039	0.021	-0.343	-1.854	0.075
2	(Constant)	6.097	1.229		4.961	<0.001
	Canton	0.052	0.037	0.238	1.394	0.174
	Gender	-0.452	0.448	-0.171	-1.010	0.321
	Age	0.442	0.211	0.344	2.099	0.045
	Sustainability-related groups	-0.036	0.020	-0.310	-1.785	0.085
3	(Constant)	5.413	1.026		5.277	<0.001
	Canton	0.055	0.037	0.254	1.493	0.146
	Age	0.435	0.211	0.339	2.066	0.048
	Sustainability-related groups	-0.031	0.019	-0.273	-1.609	0.118
4	(Constant)	6.569	0.686		9.570	<0.001
	Age	0.444	0.215	0.345	2.067	0.047
	Sustainability-related groups	-0.024	0.019	-0.206	-1.233	0.227
5	(Constant)	6.159	0.605		10.174	<0.001
	Age	0.444	0.216	0.346	2.052	0.049

a. Dependent Variable: Scoring Open Banking Financial Inclusion

Fig. 4.25 Backwards Stepwise Regression for Open Banking financial inclusion © Dr. Karen Wendt and Mathias Hauser, 2024

"Financial Inclusion", "Financial Literacy", "Transparency", "Affordability", "Efficiency", "Personalization", "Security", "Economic Growth", "Sustainability", "Innovation", "Gender Equality", or "Financial Resilience".

For the Top-Down Approach, the Data Yields some Pertinent Influences
"Sustainability-related Groups" show a significant influence on "Economic Factors", "Technological Factors", "Regulatory Factors", and "Collaboration Factors". This points to the profound influence of "Sustainability-related Groups" on these domains. Nonetheless, the analysis remains largely insignificant for "Environmental Factors", "Social Factors", and "Governance Factors", such that no significant influence can be detected.

3.7 Leapfrogging

Regarding the so-called leapfrogging of traditional banks, a majority of survey participants hold the assumption that fintechs are already positioned at various levels of leapfrogging, namely "Emerging Leapfrogging" (as reported by seven participants),

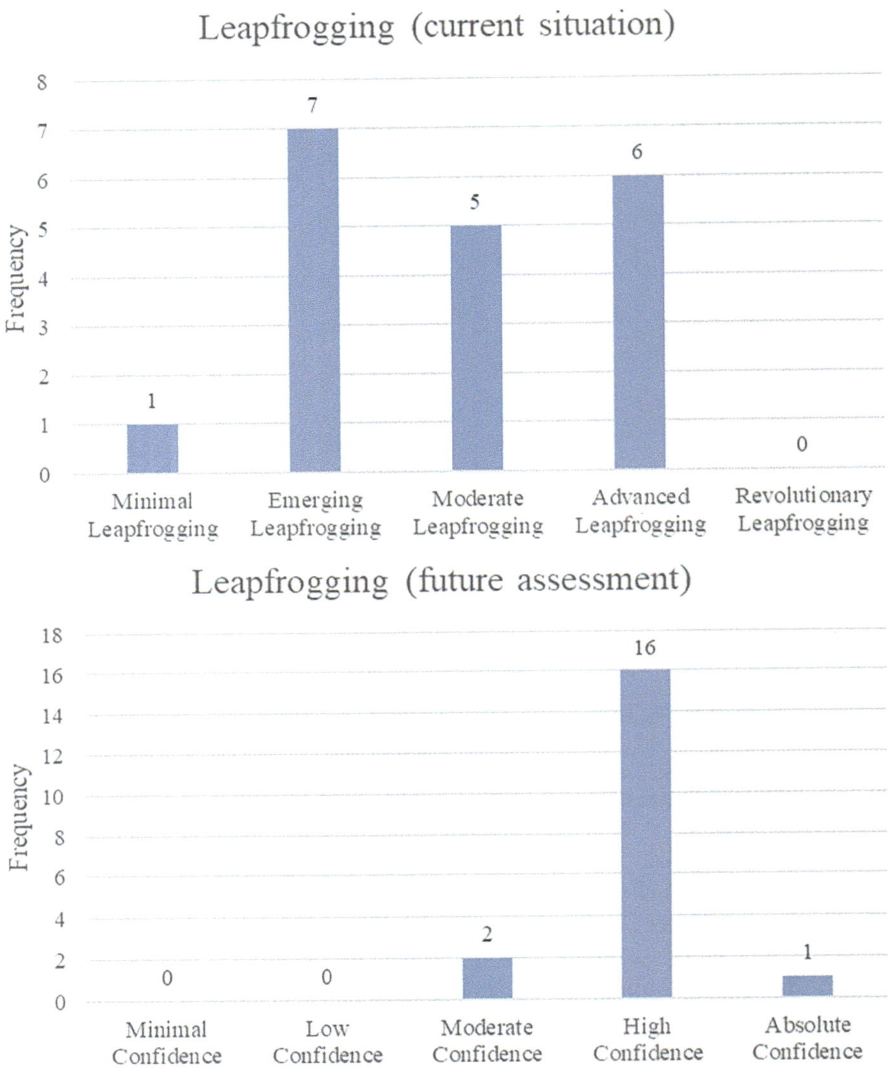

Fig. 4.26 (**a**) Leapfrogging (current situation). (**b**) Leapfrogging (future assessment). © Dr. Karen Wendt and Mathias Hauser, 2024

"Moderate Leapfrogging" (as reported by five participants), or "Advanced Leapfrogging" (as reported by six participants). These findings suggest that fintechs typically commence their endeavors by thoroughly examining and enhancing conventional banking processes to attain a competitive edge (Fig. 4.26).

In relation to the future extent of leapfrogging, a significant majority of survey participants (16 participants) express a "High Confidence" in fintechs continuing to surpass the traditional banking system. Only two participants assign a "Moderate Confidence", while a single participant allocates "Absolute Confidence".

5 Discussion and Outlook

In the following section, a thorough analysis of the study's implications is provided, evaluating the observed effects of the applied methods and identified results. Moreover, a critical reflection on the project's execution is delineated, addressing challenges encountered and lessons learned throughout the process.

1 Summary of the Results

Overall, it can be noted that the bottom-up approach scored significantly higher than the top-down approach, indicating that the impact measured for the product offering has a greater influence compared to the fintech level itself. Besides that, it becomes apparent that a significant portion of the KPIs focusing on assessing user satisfaction within the underlying Impact Themes typically exhibit inferior scores in comparison to other KPIs within the identical Impact Theme. Consequently, this observation leads to the deduction that user satisfaction alone does not serve as the predominant catalyst for generating impact.

The Bottom-up approach in Open Banking and Open Finance showed similar frequency analysis trends, with "Innovation" and "Sustainability" demonstrating exponential growth and high relevance. "Financial Inclusion", "Financial Literacy", "Transparency", "Affordability", and "Efficiency" exhibited a linear cumulative relevance trend. However, "Economic Growth", "Personalization" and "Security", had a flatter relevance trend. In contrast, it is observed that "Financial Resilience" exhibits minimal occurrence of lower scores while demonstrating a significant frequency of the "Relevant" response option, thereby indicating a substantial level of relevance. In contrast, "Gender Equality" peaked within the medium categories. A statistical t-test for independent samples was applied. Despite not perfectly aligning with Gaussian distribution, approximate normal distribution could be assumed through the Q-Q plot analysis. The Levene test indicated variance homogeneity between Open Banking and Open Finance. Through the Backward Stepwise

K. Wendt, M. Hauser, *Green FinTech*, Sustainable Finance,
https://doi.org/10.1007/978-3-031-78279-4_5

Regression algorithm, it could be established that for Open Banking, age significantly impacts "Financial Inclusion", "Financial Literacy", "Transparency", "Affordability", and "Sustainability", while canton influences "Innovation" and age and canton affect "Gender Equality" as well as "Financial Resilience". However, no significant influences were found for "Efficiency", "Personalization", "Security", and "Economic Growth". In contrast, Open Finance showed no significant influences on any assessed aspect. In the top-down approach, sustainability-related groups significantly influenced economic, technological, regulatory, and collaboration factors, but not environmental, social, and governance factors.

2 Effect Analysis

The creation of a unified impact taxonomy for Swiss fintechs, based on Impact Themes, Strategic Goals, and KPIs required a detailed analysis to understand its potential implications. The purpose of this effect analysis is to examine the process of determining these impact criteria and assess their relevance within the context of the Swiss fintech ecosystem.

The taxonomy has been constructed on a broad study based on qualitative interviews with Swiss fintech professionals in the fields of Open Banking and Open Finance, as well as ESG and Impact Specialists. These were followed by a quantitative survey to test for the validity of the taxonomy and confirm if the identified Impact Themes, Strategic Goals, and KPIs for the Swiss fintech Impact Strategy are relevant and measurable. The identified Impact Themes underline the areas in which Swiss fintechs are expected to create significant change. The analysis of such themes will aid in understanding the alignment of the needs of society and the environment, regulatory mandates, and industry trends. Analyzing such themes may also provide insights into future directions for innovation and expansion within the fintech space. The Strategic Goals outlined in the taxonomy are pivotal, serving as guiding principles for fintechs' operations and their desired impact. Assessing those objectives provides insights into their alignment with the overall goals of the fintech sector. The defined KPIs are measurable values that show how effectively fintech firms meet strategic objectives stipulated. In the context of the taxonomy, these KPIs are supposed to reflect the performance of fintechs about their impacts. The effectiveness of these KPIs lies in their ability to track progress, stimulate improvements, and ensure accountability in the industry. However, because of the scope of variety in operations and strategies that fintech companies represent, and even more so in their aspirations for impact generation, it warrants noting that the applicability and relevance of the indicators to fintech companies vary greatly.

In conclusion, the effect analysis of the impact criteria determination process explains the significance and potential implications of the proposed Impact Taxonomy for Swiss fintechs. The taxonomy's ultimate effectiveness will largely depend on its adaptation and application within the diverse landscape of the Swiss fintech industry. Future research should strive to continuously assess and refine the taxonomy, ensuring its relevance and adaptability to the evolving needs and trends in the industry.

3 Recommendations for the Financial Industry

In this chapter, the fundamental role of the designed Impact Taxonomy is elucidated and in showing how it will be applied in the strategic investment planning of asset managers and fintechs alike. It includes an exploration of how the taxonomy can systematically direct an asset managers decision-making toward fintechs that hold considerable potential for generating sustainable and socio-economic impacts. In addition, the discussion touches upon how the taxonomy enables stakeholder engagements and capacity building, assists in portfolio construction, drives product innovation, supports risk management, enriches research as well as development activities, and encourages transparency in reporting and communication. Insights from this comprehensive examination may provide significant guidance to entities in the financial market towards allowing them to harness the potential of impact-driven fintechs and redefine the landscape of Impact Investing.

Impact Investing Guide

The Impact Taxonomy is designed to be a solid guide for impact investments within the Swiss fintech landscape. It has been devised in a way that allows intricate mapping out and scoring impact drivers of fintechs, thus setting a standard within the implementation of impact practice. As fintechs begin to integrate this taxonomy into their operations market players would be equipped to recognize which firms seem well-aligned with specified impact goals. The earlier applied taxonomy for fintechs could also serve as an indicator of the commitment of these institutions to generate an optimal effect and sustainable development, making attractive investment prospects for their clients. Over time, the taxonomy could serve as a crucial tool to identify best-in-class impact fintechs, helping investors to streamline their investment decisions, thereby maximizing their impact.

Stakeholder Engagement

The Impact Taxonomy can serve as a main driver in encouraging a shared understanding of impactful fintechs. By advocating for its implementation amongst various stakeholders, financial players can stimulate a common discourse around impact-driven fintechs. The more fintechs start to implement the taxonomy, the more firms can work to synergize different stakeholders towards a cohesive approach in supporting and promoting these fintechs. The taxonomy can foster more meaningful collaborations and joint initiatives, creating an expansive impact ecosystem within the Swiss fintech industry.

Training and Capacity Building

The taxonomy provides a practical educational resource for capacity building within fintech firms. They can use the taxonomy as a roadmap to train fintech firms on the attributes and practices that characterize impactful operations. By fostering a clear understanding of the taxonomy, they can promote its widespread adoption, ensuring a standardized approach towards impact measurement within the fintech sector. This can initiate a culture of impact-oriented thinking and decision-making across the industry, hence enhancing the collective effort in driving investment with a positive impact.

Portfolio Construction

The Impact Taxonomy presents a powerful tool to assist portfolio managers in portfolio construction. As fintechs begin to adopt the taxonomy, it offers a guide for assessing the impact measurement approach of these fintechs and to determine on which perspectives (outside-in, inside-out, or inside-in) they are focused. This approach can enable portfolio managers to build a diversified portfolio of best-in-class impact fintechs, aligning their financial objectives with their commitment to driving positive impact.

Product Innovation

Fintechs can leverage the taxonomy to stimulate product innovation. As more fintechs integrate the taxonomy into their operations, it provides a wealth of insights into the sustainable practices and performance measurement of these firms. This knowledge can spark the ideation of novel sustainable and impact finance products and services. By designing financial instruments and services that resonate with the taxonomy's parameters, financial players can encourage and facilitate greater participation by fintechs in impact-driven finance practices.

Risk Management

The taxonomy can provide a comprehensive view of potential risks attached to investments. When executed, the taxonomy will, therefore, enable portfolio managers to gain a better understanding of their performance and the risks associated with their portfolios. This nuanced understanding can inform more effective strategies for asset de-risking that safeguard the financial interests of the portfolio manager while supporting fintechs during their transition toward practices that have a positive impact generation.

Research & Development

The Impact Taxonomy can serve as a robust foundation for research and development. Upon adoption of the Taxonomy by fintech firms, researchers and practitioners can continuously track their progress and shed light on their performance. These insights can guide ongoing research efforts and inform the refinement of the firm's impact.

4 Conclusions, Interpretation, and SDG-Aligned FinTech Framework

Below we provide an interpretation of the findings:

Regarding the methodological approach, it was utmost useful to combine bottom-up and top-down methodologies which allowed us to find new relevant categories from the interviews, projecting categories and KPIs not yet found in the existing literature, which circumscribe and design impact in the Swiss FinTech Taxonomy.

Bottom-up vs. top-down approaches differ as follows:

- In the bottom-up approach, KPIs were identified based on expert criteria within the fintech field from real context of best-in-class fintechs available in the field.
- The KPIs derived from the top-down approach were developed based on established themes and classification systems identified in the literature and were subsequently expanded upon.

The bottom-up approach performed better overall, suggesting that expert criteria are more aligned with real-world relevance and effectiveness than those derived solely from the literature.

Let us examine the Key Performance Indicators (KPIs) that have been identified:

Bottom-Up Approach

User Satisfaction:

KPIs assessing user satisfaction scored lower within their respective Impact Themes. This indicates that user satisfaction might not be a primary driver for impact in the fintech sector, challenging the common perception that customer satisfaction is a proxy for sustainability and overall impact. Further investigation could explore why user satisfaction is less impactful and whether there are specific contexts or sub-sectors within fintech where this is not the case.

Innovation and Sustainability:

The high relevance in the bottom-up approach is indicating these are crucial areas for fintech companies. When impact is a forward-looking approach, it is not surprising that innovation and sustainability are key areas of focus and importance. Innovations paired with sustainability have long been regarded as transformative in implementing sustainable concepts in finance and investing, and fintech can play a crucial role in this process.

In short, emphasis on innovation and sustainability reflects the industry's drive towards creating new, sustainable financial solutions. This aligns with broader industry trends where innovation is key to staying competitive, and sustainability is increasingly important due to regulatory pressures and consumer expectations.

Other Key Factors: Transparency, Affordability, Efficiency.

Financial inclusion, financial literacy, transparency, affordability, and efficiency show a linear cumulative relevance trend. While innovation and sustainability are top priorities, these other factors are also significant, albeit to a lesser extent.

Exploring specific fintech innovations that enhance financial inclusion and literacy could provide further insights into best practices and impactful solutions. Economic growth seems not to be identified as one of the relevant factors. It is worth exploring forthcoming research on why this is the case.

Financial Resilience and Gender Equality:

Financial resilience shows high relevance but lower scores, while gender equality shows medium relevance.

Despite scoring lower, financial resilience is highly relevant, indicating a gap between current performance and importance. Gender equality, while moderately relevant, indicates ongoing efforts are needed.

Initiatives to improve financial resilience and gender equality could be developed, leveraging insights from companies that excel in these areas.

Statistical Analysis:

Let us look at distribution and homogeneity:

Approximate normal distribution was assumed through Q-Q plot analysis; furthermore, the Levene test suggested variance homogeneity between Open Banking and Open Finance. The assumptions of normal distribution and variance homogeneity support the robustness of the findings. Confirmatory studies could be conducted to ensure these assumptions hold across different samples and contexts.

Regression Analysis:

Findings from the Backward Stepwise Regression suggest:

- Age significantly influences financial inclusion and literacy, as well as the transparency, affordability, and sustainability, all of which require a certain level of understanding of fintech.
- Swiss Canton: Influences innovation in Open Banking as the regional stimuli and company settlement policies vary.
- Both Age and Swiss Canton affect gender equality and financial resilience. This is an important finding, as it tells us that the Canton policies have the power to positively influence financial resilience and gender equality.
- While the data set used in the research might differ significantly from those used in other studies, as we applied not just a top-down but also a bottom-up approach to look behind the scenes and to find factors that might have been underestimated by other researchers, as they could only be found in a qualitative, bottom-up analysis. Also, differences in sample size, geographic focus, time period, and types of fintech companies examined could affect the results.
- Moreover, the high adoption rate and user behavior might have played a role.

The most important take-aways are that demographic and regional factors play significant roles in certain KPIs, suggesting tailored strategies might be necessary for different age groups and regions, also when it comes to inclusion, literacy, and affordability.

Policies and programs could be designed to address specific needs of various demographic groups and regions to enhance these KPIs effectively.

Top-down Approach Findings

With regard to Sustainability-Related Groups a significant influence and impact was found on economic, technological, regulatory, and collaboration factors, however no impact on environmental, social, and governance (ESG) factors.

Sustainability initiatives primarily drive economic and technological advancements, regulatory changes, and collaborations, but not directly ESG factors.

Integrating sustainability efforts with ESG strategies could provide a more holistic approach to achieving overall sustainability goals in fintech.

The study highlights the effectiveness of the bottom-up approach in identifying relevant KPIs in the fintech sector, with a particular emphasis on innovation and sustainability. It challenges the notion that user satisfaction is a primary driver for impact and underscores the importance of demographic and regional factors in influencing certain KPIs. The findings suggest a need for more targeted strategies to enhance financial resilience, gender equality, and other critical factors within fintech. Further research and tailored initiatives could help bridge the gaps identified and support the industry's growth and impact.

5 Project Reflection

This chapter reflects a review of the project study, methods, procedures, and steps applied. Based on the project reflection, suggestions for improvement for further project work will be presented.

Scientific Theoretical Basis

Due to the fact that Impact Investing and therefore also impact-driven fintechs are still in their infancy, it complicated the initial literature research and required a tremendous amount of scientific contribution. The implications are particularly noticeable due to the lack of a standardized and uniform impact taxonomy and due to the low number of impact-driven fintechs, which generate a measurable positive impact. Undoubtedly, the mixed-methods approach of expert interviews and personal desk research to generate an initial concept of an impact taxonomy and then testing the identified Impact Themes, Strategic Objectives, and KPIs with the aid of a quantitative survey has proven to be effective. First of all, thanks to the fintechs identified during the preliminary study, an initial overview of potential best-in-class impact fintechs could be established, which acted as a basis for the qualitative interviews. Following this, through three qualitative interviews during the preliminary study and five interviews during the main study a broad spectrum of key impact fintechs in Switzerland could be established, which was later on supplemented with an independent desk research. The selection process involved a meticulous evaluation of the best-in-class impact fintechs, taking into account their commendable implementation of impact-oriented strategies throughout their operational framework. In order to encompass a more comprehensive array of viewpoints within the Swiss fintech landscape, the sample was expanded to encompass additional fintech companies as identified in the IFZ fintech Study 2023, which yielded a robust and heterogeneous sample.

Reflection on the Study Approach

In the course of writing the study, the authors have learned a great deal about the current state of Impact investing as well as Impact measurement within the Swiss fintech landscape and gained insights for potential approaches for defining a taxonomy. Due to the initial literature research, a vast understanding of relevant studies could be established, which acted as a guidance for the later phase of the research. Besides that, due to an early set-up of the project plan, a timely execution could be accomplished, and the achievement of milestones could be checked utilizing controls. The implementation of the interviews and quantitative survey generally adhered to the outlined plan; however, certain challenges were encountered. These included delays in identifying suitable interview partners, which consequently led to a postponement of the project timeline. Additionally, the configuration of the quantitative online survey required a longer duration than initially anticipated, resulting in an increased workload. Furthermore, the analysis of the survey data also demanded more time than projected. Nevertheless, upon reflection, the chosen approach for this project work can be deemed suitable and appropriate.

Glossary

Cybersecurity The process of creating, implementing, and employing technologies, procedures, and practices to safeguard corporate resources, customer information, and intellectual property from malicious or accidental intrusions by unauthorized persons.

ESG (Environmental, Social, and Governance) A set of criteria, launched by the United Nations in 2006, in order to determine a company's sustainable behavior, which socially responsible investors use to evaluate potential investments.

Green Fintech Fintechs, which operate with the aim of reducing climate change risks in emerging and developing nations in order to implement the Paris Agreement and to support the accomplishment of the Sustainable Development Goals.

Impact Investing Investments with the main intention to generate measurable positive social, environmental or governance related impact along with generating financial returns.

Open Banking A banking practice that provides application programming interfaces (APIs) to third-party financial service providers with an open access to customer banking, transaction, and other financial data from banks and non-bank financial companies.

Open Finance The ability to access financial data and take action on it in order to create customized experiences, accelerate innovation, and promote industry cooperation.

SDGs (Sustainable Development Goals) A worldwide agenda for 2030 with 17 goals for sustainable development, which for the first time cover all three dimensions of sustainability (social, environmental, economic).

K. Wendt, M. Hauser, *Green FinTech*, Sustainable Finance,
https://doi.org/10.1007/978-3-031-78279-4

References

Adel, I. (2023, February 22). *Leveraging Fintech to drive financial inclusion: Strategies and best practices*. Forbes. https://www.forbes.com/sites/forbestechcouncil/2023/02/22/leveraging-fintech-to-drive-financial-inclusion-strategies-and-best-practices/

Ankenbrand, T. (2022). *IFZ Fintech study 2022—An overview of Swiss FinTech*. https://hub.hslu.ch/retailbanking/wp-content/uploads/sites/7/2022/03/IFZ-FinTech-Study-2022.pdf

Ankenbrand, T., Bieri, D., Kronenberger, T., & Reichmuth, L. (2023). *IFZ FinTech study 2023: An overview of Swiss FinTech*. https://hub.hslu.ch/retailbanking/download/ifz-fintech-study/

B Lab. (2022). *We are excited to share that in 2023, we will be re-envisioning our analytics capabilities into a new, more integrated product*. Analytics. https://www.bcorporation.net/en-us/programs-and-tools/analytics

B Lab. (2024). *B impact assessment*. https://www.bcorporation.net/en-us/programs-and-tools/b-impact-assessment

B Lab Global. (2023, May 15). *Preliminary consultation suggests new B Corp standards are ambitious yet attainable*. https://www.bcorporation.net/en-us/news/press/preliminary-consultation-suggests-new-b-corp-standards-are-ambitious-yet-attainable

Blakstad, S. (2018). FinTech revolution: Universal inclusion in the new financial ecosystem. In *FinTech revolution universal inclusion in the new financial ecosystem* (1st ed.). Springer International Publishing.

Bugg-Levine, A., & Emerson, J. (2011). Impact investing: Transforming how we make money while making a difference. *Innovations (Cambridge, Mass.), 6*(3), 9–18.

Clarkin, J. E., & Cangioni, L. (2016). Impact investing: A primer and review of the literature. *Entrepreneurship Research Journal, 6*(2), 135–173.

Dahms, A. K., Busch, T., Döbeli, S., Hess, K., Laville, J., & Bodenmann, A. (2019). *Swiss sustainable investment market study 2019* (p. 76). https://www.sustainablefinance.ch/api/rm/X4GU5NP7QYQ76FZ/2019-06-03-ssf-swiss-sustainable-investment-market.pdf

Demir, A., Pesqué-Cela, V., Altunbas, Y., & Murinde, V. (2022). Fintech, financial inclusion and income inequality: A quantile regression approach. *The European Journal of Finance, 28*(1), 86–107.

Demirgüç-Kunt, A., Klapper, L., Singer, D., Ansar, S., & Hess, J. (2018). *The Global Findex database 2017: Measuring financial inclusion and the Fintech revolution*. World Bank Group. https://openknowledge.worldbank.org/entities/publication/ed800062-e062-5a05-acdd-90429d8a5a07

Dorfleitner, G., Hornuf, L., Schmitt, M., & Weber, M. (2017). Definition of FinTech and description of the FinTech industry. In *FinTech in Germany* (pp. 5–10). Springer International Publishing.

Eccles, R. G., Lee, L.-E., & Stroehle, J. C. (2020). The social origins of ESG: An analysis of innovest and KLD. *Organization & Environment, 33*(4), 575–596.

K. Wendt, M. Hauser, *Green FinTech*, Sustainable Finance,
https://doi.org/10.1007/978-3-031-78279-4

Erchinger, R. (2022). *ESG(e)-Kriterien—Die Schlüssel Zum Aufbau Einer Nachhaltigen Unternehmensführung: Eine Eignungsanalyse Ausgewählter Standardkriterien*. In *ESG(e)-Kriterien—Die Schlüssel Zum Aufbau Einer Nachhaltigen Unternehmensführung: Eine Eignungsanalyse Ausgewählter Standardkriterien*. Springer Fachmedien Wiesbaden GmbH.

European Parliament and the Council of the European Union. (2014). *Directive 2014/52/ EU of the European parliament and of the council* (p. 18). https://eur-lex.europa.eu/legal-content/EN/TXT/PDF/?uri=CELEX:32014L0052&from=EN

GIIN. (2011). *Improving livelihoods, removing barriers: Investing for impact in Mtanga Farms*. (p. 10) [Case Study]. https://thegiin.org/assets/documents/pub/improving-livelihoods-removing-barriers-investing-for-impact.pdf

GIIRS. (2012). *GIIRS | What GIIRS does*. https://giirs.org/about-giirs/about

Global Impact Investing Network. (2019). *IRIS+ and the five dimensions of impact* (p. 9). Global Impact Investing Network. https://iris.thegiin.org/document/iris-and-the-five-dimensions/

Global Impact Investing Network. (2020). *What you need to know about impact investing*. GIIN. https://thegiin.org/impact-investing/need-to-know/

Global Impact Investing Network. (2022). *IRIS+ and the SDGs* (p. 73). Global Impact Investing Network. https://iris.thegiin.org/document/iris-and-the-sdgs/

Gottschlich, D., & Friedrich, B. (2014). The legacy of Sylvicultura oeconomica. A critical reflection on the notion of sustainability. *Das Erbe der Sylvicultura oeconomica. Eine kritische Reflexion des Nachhaltigkeitsbegriffs. Gaia (Heidelberg, Germany), 23*(1), 23–29.

Greenhouse Gas Protocol. (2013). *Technical guidance for calculating Scope 3 emissions* (p. 182). https://ghgprotocol.org/sites/default/files/standards/Scope3_Calculation_Guidance_0.pdf

Hauff, V. (Ed.). (1987). *Our common future—Report of the world commission on environment and development*. Eggenkamp.

Langley, P., & Leyshon, A. (2021). The platform political economy of FinTech: Reintermediation, consolidation and capitalisation. *New Political Economy, 26*(3), 376–388.

Loy, A., Follett, L., & Hofmann, H. (2016). Variations of Q-Q plots: The power of our eyes. *The American Statistician, 70*(2), 202–214.

McCarthy, K., Emme, L., & Glasgo, L. (2022). *IRIS+ thematic taxonomy* (p. 43). Global Impact Investing Network. https://iris.thegiin.org/document/iris-thematic-taxonomy/

Morgan, R. K. (2012). Environmental impact assessment: The state of the art. *Impact Assessment and Project Appraisal, 30*(1), 5–14.

MSCI. (2022). *MSCI ESG ratings methodology*. https://www.msci.com/documents/1296102/-21901542/ESG-Ratings-Methodology-Exec-Summary.pdf

Mudaliar, A., & Dithrich, H. (2019). *Sizing the impact investing market* (p. 16). https://thegiin.org/assets/Sizing%20the%20Impact%20Investing%20Market_webfile.pdf

Oliver Wyman Forum. (2021). *There's no low-carbon future without cutting Scope 3 emissions*. https://climateactionnavigator.oliverwymanforum.com/scope-3-emissions

Puschmann, T., Hoffmann, C. H., & Khmarskyi, V. (2020). How green fintech can alleviate the impact of climate change—The case of Switzerland. *Sustainability (Basel, Switzerland), 12*(24), 1–28.

Streefkerk, R. (2019, April 18). *Inductive vs. Deductive research approach (with examples)*. Scribbr. https://www.scribbr.com/methodology/inductive-deductive-reasoning/

United Nations Conference on Environment and Development. (1992). *Convention on biological diversity* (p. 28). https://www.cbd.int/doc/legal/cbd-en.pdf

Vergara, C. C., & Agudo, L. F. (2021). Fintech and sustainability: Do they affect each other? *Sustainability (Basel, Switzerland), 13*(7012), 19.

Verheem, R. A. A., & Tonk, J. A. M. N. (2000). Strategic environmental assessment: One concept, multiple forms. *Impact Assessment and Project Appraisal, 18*(3), 177–182.

Wendt, K. (2018). Positive impact investing: A sustainable bridge between strategy, innovation, change and learning. In *Positive impact investing a sustainable bridge between strategy, innovation, change and learning* (1st ed.). Springer International Publishing.

Wendt, K. (2022, November 22). *Eccos international*. http://eccosinternational.io/english/. http://eccosinternational.io/english/

Zurbriggen, L., Kohler, F., Dröge, K., & Hodel, M. (2018). *Qualitative Interviews meistern (1. Auflage)*. Cornelsen Verlag GmbH.

Index

K. Wendt, M. Hauser, *Green FinTech*, Sustainable Finance,
https://doi.org/10.1007/978-3-031-78279-4

MIX
Papier aus verantwortungsvollen Quellen
Paper from responsible sources
FSC® C105338

If you have any concerns about our products,
you can contact us on
ProductSafety@springernature.com

In case Publisher is established outside the EU,
the EU authorized representative is:
Springer Nature Customer Service Center GmbH
Europaplatz 3, 69115 Heidelberg, Germany

Printed by Libri Plureos GmbH
in Hamburg, Germany